12-15-11

EARTHLY ANGELS

EARTHLY ANGELS

David Chen's Survival of Famine and Persecution

By Phyllis A. Milkon

Burgess Creative Ventures

Publishing Division, Bend, Oregon

Published by:
Burgess Creative Ventures
Publishing Division
P.O. Box 5005
Bend, OR 97708-5005

Printed in the USA by:
Old Paths Tract Society, Shoals, Indiana

ISBN 0-9630025-2-X

3 5 7 9 10 8 6 4 2

Library of Congress Catalog Card Number: 99-94318

I dedicate this book to

my parents, Harvey and Toni Milkon,

who courageously

risked their own personal safety

in order to bring

their "precious cargo" to China.

and

I also dedicate this book to

David Chen's Japanese grandchildren.

Ai Ai, To To and Yu Yu.

As an illustration of God's love and blessings.

"Train a child in the way he should go, and
when he is old he will not turn from it." Pro. 22:6

Foreword

David Chen is the most humble man that I have ever met. It has been a privilege to tell his story so that his Japanese grandchildren and others can learn how God protected him from famine and persecution in China and brought him to political asylum and retirement in the USA. David's Chinese name has been withheld for his protection.

During personal interviews and telephone conversations, David and I have become very close. I prayed with him when he had cataract surgery on his only good eye and thought he might go blind. We also praised God when he received his pacemaker.

When writing about the Red Guard period, I suddenly realized that David and I had each walked through "the valley of the shadow of death" at the same time. Thirty years ago, he was imprisoned, subjected to cruel beatings and in total despair attempted suicide. I suffered a nervous breakdown and was diagnosed with manic depressive illness. In our pain, each of us called out to God, and He answered our prayers. We agree that without our faith neither of us would be alive today.

This book is an attempt to glorify God by showing the miracles that God performed in David's life. Throughout this fascinating story, you will see when God held his hand, crossed his path with earthly angels or simply carried him, when life proved too cruel.

This book uses the new Chinese names, with the old name in brackets on its first occurrence, because newer names may be more familiar to the reader. With the exception, that it was necessary to use old names for small towns and villages, where it was not clear what the new names were.

Acknowledgments

Earthly Angels is based on many interviews with David Chen, conversations with others that were involved in some of the events, and materials supplied by the organizations that touched his life. Materials and photographs used in this book have been reprinted with their permission.

We wish to thank the following persons for their interest in this project and immediate response for requested materials. They saved many months of research time. It has been a blessing to work with each of them.

Mr. Alfred Lackey, President of Kids Alive International, formerly Home of Onesiphorus, for reviewing the final manuscript. Rev. Gus Stralnic, Church and Human Relations, for providing a wealth of information including *Helping China's Helpless Ones to Help Themselves, Repairing the Breach, 20th Century Onesiphorus* and past issues of *The Harvester* magazine. I am especially thankful for his trusting me with several out of print publications, which turned out to be vital links to the story. Also, Mrs. Louise Rock, Publications Editor, for taking the time to edit the manuscript and make helpful recommendations.

In memory of Mr. George Hedberg, past Director of Home of Onesiphorus, for his enthusiasm on this project. Unfortunately, Mr. Hedberg passed away before he could fulfill his promise to edit this book. We wish to thank his family for providing past letters from David, which he had saved. David had forgotten many details that they helped to clarify.

Dr. George Sweeting, Chancellor, Moody Bible Institute, for his gift of several books that describe the institute and its founder, *Lessons from the Life of Moody, Teaching The Word Reaching The World (Moody Bible*

Institute The First 100 Years), and A Passion For Souls (The Life of D.L. Moody). Also, many thanks to his secretary, Joanna Zarriello, who helped with many details and Heidy Hartley, Public Relations Department, who supplied information.

Rev. Allen Finley, former president of CNEC, now Partners International, for his numerous phone calls to clarify David's story. Also, for the personal photographs he supplied. Arthur and Betty Gee, Coordinator of Southeast Asia Department and Esther Fan, Director Chinese Relations in the US, for supplying various materials and encouragement.

Peter Willard, Director of Chop Point Inc., his wife, Jean, and his daughter-in-law, Wendy, for the information and photos they supplied.

David and I would also like to thank everyone who donated their time, reviewed the book and gave us their comments. They include: Elinor Hoole and Patricia Haaby for general content, Paul Hamley for the song, and Pastors Jack Dunaway, Gil Miller and Daniel LeLaCheur for religious material. Also, a very special thank-you to Bonnie and Bob Baldwin, for editing this manuscript, Lena Hurst, for computer consulting and design. Leonard Peoples, for use of computer equipment and Jeffrey Maul, for photography.

In addition, thanks to those persons unknown who supplied the Chinese Bibles and Christian books that were delivered to David in China and made this story possible.

Every effort was taken to make this story as accurate as possible but occasionally it was necessary to choose between several versions of the same event. In cases like these, David's preference was given sole consideration.

Contents

Contents continued

1

Recollections

A small starving child sifted through the dirt for anything to fill his swollen belly. If he were lucky, he might find a few grains of wheat or some wild herbs. He was desperate for anything to appease his hunger. The farmer, who owned the small plot of land, saw him and was furious. His wheat field was not ready for harvest and there were so many starving children. The farmer's heart was not softened by the pleading eyes and emaciated body wrapped in rags. He grabbed the pesky three year old and slapped him repeatedly for ruining his crop. The child shrieked in terror until he was able to slip out of the farmer's grasp. Then he ran with his heart pounding and tears streaming down his face, cutting his bare feet on stones and twigs as he fled. Out of the farmer's sight, he fell to the ground and cried himself to sleep. This was a beating he would never forget.

The child's mother did not come to his defense. Days earlier, she had gone to town never to return. His father found work as best he could, but he was often absent for days at a time. His older sister couldn't help him either. Four years older, she had been sent to the next town where she helped as an "amah" or nanny to the children of American missionaries.

These are the earliest recollections of "David" Chen, whose Chinese name has been withheld for his protection. He chose the name, David, after becoming a Christian. The remarkable journey of David's life spans more than ninety years. Through famine, persecution, and close encounters with death, he attempted to follow God's plan for his life. To make all of this possible, God supplied many miracles and a host of heavenly and earthly angels.

2

Asleep on the Hay

David Chen was born in 1908 in Tsi-li-chuang, a small isolated village in the Jiangsu [Kiangsu] Province where Mandarin was the local dialect. In this part of Northern China the land was primarily used for dry farming as opposed to the wet farming needed for rice. In normal years, farmers produced a main crop of winter wheat along with a small, secondary crop of millet. Now, there was a terrible famine and to avoid starvation, people were forced to eat grass, tender leaves from trees or tree bark.

There were few houses and no school in this rural area, and economic conditions were harsh for everyone. Times were so bad that it was not unusual for parents, who could not cope, to abandon their children, commit suicide, or even destroy their entire families.

David's mother, Sun-sze Chen, could not cope with the misery and starvation around her. His only memory of her is the day she went to town and never came home. Neither he nor his sister, Ruilan, ever knew what happened to her, although rumors occasionally surfaced of her remarriage or death.

His father, Hsiu-shan Chen, was a farmer but he did not own any land. When the famine became worse, he went to Jining [Tsining] in the Shandong [Shantung] Province and became a guard at the Presbyterian mission. Jining was a much larger city which had many buildings. Commerce flourished because merchants could

3

transport their goods by boat on the Grand Canal. While working with the missionaries, Hsiu-shan became a Christian. He was the first person from his village to do so, and this was obvious to others, because he cut off his queue (pigtail).

Politically, times were changing rapidly and radically. It was the last years of the Manchu (Qing) dynasty, and reformers such as Sun Yatsen were calling for an end to the monarchy. The Manchu dynasty ruled China from 1644 to 1911. Its collapse signaled the last of Imperial China.

A provisional government–the Nationalist Party–was formed and briefly led by Sun Yatsen. By 1916, the new government failed and the country was broken up into a series of fiefdoms. There was no established authority over the majority of the country, and warlords and their troops fought ruthlessly for power and territory. The warlords were supreme military leaders with no interest in justice. There had never been a proper legal system, and justice was often at the whim of an official. Now, corruption was rampant and old institutions collapsed. There would be no clear political leader until the Communists gained control, over thirty years later. In the turmoil of the current times, most people were totally occupied with survival.

The years after his father left were very difficult for David. He was destitute, always hungry, and he spent his days going from house to house begging for food. He was happy for the smallest morsel. The famine was so severe that he could not even search the garbage for something to eat because there was none. Nothing was thrown away especially food. During this time, he lived with distant relatives and slept on their dirt floor. From time to time, he asked about his father but no one knew how he was. One day, when he was about four years old, his grand uncle put this frail child in a wheelbarrow and pushed him about thirty miles north to Jining. Although he pitied David, he was anxious to get rid of an extra mouth to feed. They searched for his father, and when they found him, his grand uncle returned home alone. David remained with his father for several years.

In order to earn a living, his father became a wheelbarrow pusher. This was a type of taxi that preceded the rickshaw puller. First, it was his own business, and he worked day and night whenever he could get a job. He was often out of town for two or three days at a time. David and his father often had no money and many times nothing to eat. Food, when available, was only a meager gruel. Just outside the compound of the Presbyterian mission, there was a primitive inn where hospital patients stayed. David and his father lived there, but not in one of the small rooms. They lived with the animals where they slept on the hay. The hay served both as bedding and as a blanket. They were more fortunate than others who were forced to sleep outdoors. When his father was away, David slept there alone.

Conditions improved when his father was hired by the missionaries to deliver goods from the city to the country. Then, his small salary enabled him to buy food on a more regular basis and, when necessary, to buy on account from other merchants. Now David could get food when his father was out of town.

For a few years, while he was in Jining, David had the opportunity to attend the elementary school founded by the Presbyterian mission. Here he learned about Jesus. In addition to the Presbyterians, other denominations had missions in other parts of the city.

One night, when his father was away, eight year old David fell asleep on the hay as usual and had a vivid dream. A magnificent figure in a white, fur robe was standing in a boat high in the sky. The boat slowly descended from Heaven to the water where David was standing in a small boat belonging to an uncle. The figure said, "Do you want to go with Me?" Confused by the stranger and not knowing who he was, David timidly answered, "No." Then, the figure returned to Heaven by boat. Later in the dream, he asked his uncle about this and his uncle explained the figure was Jesus. At this point, David woke up. He looked around at the straw and the animals and remembered he was alone in the stable. This was his first encounter with Jesus. Much later when he saw a poster of Jesus, as a shepherd, he realized that this was the same person he had seen in his dream!

3

To China with Love

Leslie Anglin grew up in Georgia in a strong Christian family. On several occasions his life was spared, and his mother told him it was because God had important plans for him. In addition to teaching him to have a strong love for God, she was also instrumental in getting him to recognize the needs of others. At an early age, he decided to become a missionary to China and eventually he became a business man to finance his calling.

Ava Patton was orphaned at the age of five. She and her siblings were placed in the Thornwell Seminary, a Presbyterian School, later called the Thornwell Orphanage. At Thornwell, in Clinton, South Carolina, she lived, was educated and later graduated.

Ava met Leslie Anglin and their friendship grew into a deep love. They were married in 1904. After living in Albany, Georgia, for two years, they moved to New Mexico. Then, for three years, they were missionaries in Mexico. Upon returning to New Mexico, they met Rev. T. L. Blalock, a "faith" missionary, who trusted God to supply his needs and whose missionary efforts were not sponsored by any group. Blalock told them about the needs of the Chinese people, and after much prayer and consideration, the Anglins also decided to step out in faith.

In 1910, they said goodbye to relatives and friends, many for the last time, and sailed to China. When they arrived, Rev. Blalock met them at Tsingtao. They traveled by train from Tsingtao to Jining where he showed them around the city. The Anglins saw the marks of starvation on the many poor people and it touched their hearts. Blalock took them to their new home in Taian. It was an arduous journey. They traveled on rough, bumpy, country roads sitting in springless wheelbarrows. Arriving in Taian, they were introduced to their new living quarters, a simple structure with a dirt floor and a crudely made table with benches. Deeply disturbed by the starving people they had seen, the Anglins bowed their heads in front of the simple meal God had provided and thanked Him for bringing them to this needy land.

In the beginning, they spent most of their time learning the difficult language and adapting to the local customs. Before long, they were conversing with others and eating with chopsticks. In years to come Anglin became so fluent he even dreamed in Chinese.

A few months after their arrival, Ava gave birth to a baby girl. She soon became the delight of their lives. Every new experience with Margaret Evelyn was a treasured moment because they had wanted a child for a long time. They hoped to show the Chinese a loving, Christian family.

Life was hard but as soon as their language skills improved, they pushed all their energies into evangelistic crusades, going from village to village telling people about Jesus. It was during this time that Anglin became convinced of the need for Chinese Christians to preach the gospel to their own people. In 1912, he organized a mission in Taian for this purpose.

In September of 1912, joy turned to deep sorrow when their sixteen-month-old baby died. If they had been in the United States, a doctor may have been able to save their beloved daughter, but in this primitive place nothing could be done.

Time passed, and they continued to work hard developing the mission. The work helped to offset some of the sorrow on the loss of their daughter. On one of their trips to a local village, they had several encounters with a small, beggar boy, Lieu. They decided to take him in. Soon a widow and three boys came to them for assistance. Leslie and Ava prayed to God for money to help them.

After one prayer session, Leslie had a vision in which God revealed to him a sign over the gate in front of their home. The sign said "Home of Onesiphorus." Also, Leslie saw himself receiving a long stream of boys and girls, and men and women who were poor, hungry and in need of assistance. Leslie looked up "Onesiphorus." He found that the Apostle Paul had said, "May the Lord show mercy to the household of Onesiphorus, because he often refreshed me and was not ashamed of my chains [while Paul was imprisoned in Rome]." 2 Tim. 1:16 As Onesiphorus was able to show kindness to Paul, the Anglins wanted to demonstrate this Christian caring, by helping impoverished Chinese children, men and women. The Anglins continued to pray and think about this new idea. Then, they realized that an orphanage would enable them to train children for their long range plan. The official opening of "Home of Onesiphorus" was in 1916.

At times Anglin was criticized for giving up evangelistic work for the children's home, but they never gave it up. He and his wife continued with the long range plan of training Christians to be the heart of self-supporting native churches. He felt that by helping the destitute, he was laying the groundwork for God to do mighty things and, therefore, the accomplishment would be greater than anything that could be done by he or his wife alone.

In the beginning, many letters were written to solicit support for the new work. As their family continued to grow, he started *The Harvester* magazine. In the beginning, it was written and published in China and mailed all over the world to thousands–predominately Americans. These supporters prayed and sent donations.

Leslie Anglin ran the children's home very efficiently. The Home grew, many buildings were built, and almost twenty acres of land were available for farming. Although an increasing number of Christians sent donations, it seemed they never had enough money. With supporters half way around the world, drought, floods, famine, wars and rumors of wars, the Anglins put their trust in God and He supplied their needs.

Leslie Anglin prayed to God for direction. Modeling on American school methods, he hired local teachers to teach the children to read and write. Also, he planned many projects that would help toward making the home self-supporting. He was very industrious and most things were done on the grounds. The Home was divided into many departments each with a supervisor who had one or more instructors. The children were taught many trades. Girls learned to knit, crochet and sew. They made the clothes and patched any torn garments. Boys built structures using mud bricks and stones and made wood furniture. They did repairs including roofing and tinsmithing. Some were taught weaving, tailoring or shoemaking. Others prepared the grounds for gardens. When the children made more products than the home could use, they were sold to offset expenses.

In the beginning, light at the Home was from kerosene lamps. Later on, Anglin purchased a generator to power the lights and machines. He set up a mill which ground flour for the Home. Also, he was able to make a profit by charging the peasants a small fee to grind their flour.

The Anglins taught by setting a good example. The children respected them, loved them, and considered them their father and mother. After graduation, many stayed on as instructors and supervisors.

4

David Comes "Home"

David's sister lived in the girls' dormitory of the elementary school which was part of the Presbyterian mission in Jining. Although boys were not allowed, he managed a few visits with her. One thing he realized was that she had food and he did not.

One day while his father was working, David sat on a doorstep. He was quite faint. Someone felt sorry for this sickly child and gave him some steamed bread. Immediately, he felt better. Starvation was a constant problem in China, and it was not uncommon for parents to bring their children to an orphanage rather than watch them starve. David decided this would be best for him and discussed it with his father who did not want him to go, but David insisted. He had heard about the free food, free shelter, free clothes and the school. David found all of this very appealing. He asked a neighbor to take him to the children's home on his next visit to see his daughter.

In 1920, when David Chen arrived at the "Home of Onesiphorus," he was twelve years old. Leslie Anglin told David he needed someone to sign an authorization for him to stay at the Home. His neighbor agreed to sign the paper, and a new world of opportunities opened up for him. At the time of his arrival, there were about 200 children. David's first delight was to find out that there were two meals a day. Jianbing (a type of thin pancake) and gruel were wonderful for the hungry children.

13

David's day was divided into a half day of work and a half day of school. Anglin felt that all children should learn a trade to support themselves. The boys and girls went to separate schools.

All boys and girls were placed into smaller groups that shared a dorm and the older children were responsible for helping the younger ones. Each dorm had about twelve boys or girls plus a monitor. David was assigned to one of the boys' dorms. He found out that "the bed" was one large platform of clay bricks wide enough for twelve children. There was another smaller bed for the monitor. This allowed them to sleep just above the dirt floor. David was given a small straw mat to place on the clay bricks and a little quilt to cover himself.

Prayer and Bible studies were very important. Anglin taught the children to depend on God, not himself, for their smallest needs. David learned to trust God and understand how God answers prayer. Also, he witnessed many miracles. He watched the Anglins pray desperately for food, clothing, or other things and he saw how God supplied those needs. Over time, David's faith grew and he became a Christian. He chose to celebrate December 25th, the birthday of Jesus, as his birthday because he did not know his own.

In addition, Anglin taught the children to pray out loud together for God's help. For many years, there was no clinic or hospital, so Anglin depended on God to take care of the children. David, like many of the other children, suffered through measles, chicken pox, scabies and other illnesses. Anglin had no medical background, and there were some health problems until proper sanitation techniques could be applied. This was minor compared to saving the lives of hundreds of starving Chinese children.

At one point David got an eye infection that was eventually cured.

David and the other young children carried stones from the mountainside to build the dormitories. When he went out of the compound alone, David sometimes had the opportunity to go to the mountains. Even before he knew what salvation was, he felt closer to God in the mountains then anywhere else. He would pray to God and would ask Him for help. God answered David's prayers.

One of his first jobs was weaving. He learned to use a spindle to form and twist yarn. As he got older, he was expected to use the yarn to weave cloth for clothes. David worked the loom but was intimidated by a harsh instructor. His fear caused his work to be inferior. Then one night while he was sleeping David saw a visual image of the loom and how to work the different parts. He thanked God for answering his prayers because from that night forward he could work the loom as professionally as any other boy. The instructor was amazed. On a good day, with no machine failures, he produced forty to fifty feet of cloth. The Home also made hospital gauze which was of the highest quality and sold to a local hospital.

Anglin considered David very dependable. When he got older it was his job to run from the Home on the east side through the city of Taian to the post office on the west side, to get the mail. Traveling quickly through the city, he never stopped to play. He brought the mail back in a sack and placed it on Anglin's desk. Anglin was very happy to get any mail, because it usually contained checks or donor slips and the very survival of the children's home depended upon these funds. David was always glad to be useful. Later, he helped Anglin in his office, was taught some English by Mrs. Anglin and was able to do some typing for Anglin. Because he was honest, David also helped with keeping track of the money. One day, money was missing and David was very upset because he was the only one with access to it. As hard as he tried, he could not figure out what happened to it. He was deeply disturbed. That night in a dream, he saw an open ledger book, and God gave him an explanation. He saw the incorrect entries and realized that there was no missing money. It was an accounting mistake! When David saw Anglin the next day, he was able to show him the entries, explain the errors, and restore the confidence that had been placed in him.

When David was seventeen, his father visited because he was in the area. As a wheelbarrow pusher, his father was responsible for taking Presbyterian missionaries to rural areas where they gave out food. Also, missionaries often came to Taian for vacation because it was near Taishan which was cooler because of the mountains. This time they were only passing through. David's father had not seen him in five years nor sent any letters, because he was uneducated and illiterate. David's father was pleased that he was grown up and that he had been well fed.

Since the visit was for a few days, his father took him to town to a communal bath for men. It was David's first! At the children's home, he washed occasionally out of the small basin of water he shared with twelve other children, but water was too scarce for the luxury of a bath. When David's father rubbed his back with a wash rag, this simple gesture was the first demonstration of love he had ever received. David was happy that his father was very pleased with him. In the Chinese way, it was a nonverbal approval. David was glad that he had at least one parent.

David's sister, Ruilan, did not come to the Home of Onesiphorus, because she could not leave her job. Once while in Taishan, she sent a message to David and asked him to visit her, which he did. At this time, the Home did not have enough food for all the children. Ruilan gave him some leftover bread. Hungry, he did not hesitate to eat it, even though the top was covered with mold.

During David's years in Taian, the warlords and their fief system collapsed and China was ruled by the Nationalists under General Chiang Kaishek. To give the government a mark of stability, the capital was moved from its current site in the North, Beijing [Peking], to the South at Nanjing [Nanking]. In the Spring of 1927, there was a civil war in the South, Nanjing fell, and several foreigners were murdered. Many missionaries left the area but the Anglins stayed on to take care of their growing family. A major problem was the disruption in mail deliveries. The uprising calmed down, but money was needed for food and supplies. While Ava stayed behind to take care of the Home, it was necessary for Anglin to go the United States for fund-raising.

Rev. Leslie Anglin left China in 1928 and visited hundreds of churches, assemblies and organizations in 48 states, then went traveling through Scandinavian countries, Europe, and the Near East. He also made a special visit to his boyhood dream, Palestine. He returned to China in November of 1929. During his trip, Anglin spoke about ministering to needy souls physically and spiritually. He believed in showing strength and love of God, spreading the wonderful message of the Cross and raising up Christians to go back to their people with the gospel message. He spoke of the needs of China and pleaded with people to open their hearts and help the starving

17

Chinese. It was during this time that G. A. Lundmark and his wife, Florence, became interested in the work. A Chicago office was opened in 1928. Lundmark, a businessman, was able to help with activities for the Home. He collected funds and sent them to China.

When his ship arrived in Shanghai, Anglin was delighted to find his wife waiting for him. Ava had left two senior boys in charge of the Home which now had about 600 children. For ten days, the Anglins were able to relax and visit friends and business acquaintances. But while the Anglins were gone, a girl ran back to her village. The senior boys blamed David for this, because he and the girl came from the same town and because he had helped her once, when she was sick. Actually, the brother of one of the senior boys had helped her jump over the wall. The senior boys punished David and made a big fuss. They forced David to leave and also fired a teacher.

David was about twenty-one years old when he left. He had been at the Home nine years, because he had worked in the office after graduation. David credits the Home of Onesiphorus for saving him from starvation and giving him the opportunity to learn about Jesus. He never forgot the kindness he received from the Anglins.

5

Seminary

David left Taian and returned to Jining where he hoped to find his family. His father was working elsewhere with Presbyterian missionaries and his sister was in another city learning how to be a kindergarten teacher. This was disappointing news. David met Kuan, the teacher that was fired from the Home by the senior boys. She was a friend of Miss Grace Nicholson.

Grace Nicholson had been a missionary and helper at the Home of Onesiphorus and she had taught David typing and office work. She sent a letter to the Presbyterian missionaries to find out if they had seen David and if he wanted to go to Bible college. At this point in his life, with no job, no available relatives, and no friends, he gladly accepted. Although, he did not even know where he was going, he looked forward to this new opportunity to serve God!

The North China Theological Seminary was started by the Presbyterian mission in Tengxian [Tenghsian]. One of the earliest schools, it was very large and graduated many preachers that later became famous. Miss Nicholson arranged for David to be accepted and sent money for his support. David had to complete two years pre-college then two years of seminary studies. After attending this school for four years he graduated in June, 1933.

At the seminary David became acquainted with Oscar Walton, a missionary who taught English. He taught David

English and David taught him Chinese. They became roommates and David had the luxury of sharing his part of the Western style house, where the professors lived. For David these were deluxe accommodations which included throw rugs, running water, a bathtub and beds. David appreciated this arrangement and sometimes helped his friend with typing.

While there David and another teacher, Professor Steven, became friends. Prof. Steven was called to the Jiangsu mission field, and he contacted David. For a short while in 1936, David helped him and gained some experience in the field. This proved useful when David began his ministries.

Another significant figure in David's life was Miss Dodds. She was a Presbyterian missionary that ran a girls' school on the same compound as the seminary. She knew a school girl, Yushin Chen, and took on the role of matchmaker. Miss Dodds told David about Yushin's background and, in the Chinese way, formally introduced the couple.

Yushin was a country girl who came from an unbeliever family. She was interested in getting an education and liked being in the city where she attended the Christian Middle School. Her relatives were upset that she was attending a Christian school. When they found out that a missionary was trying to match her with a seminary graduate, who was six years older, they were absolutely furious. After David and Yushin became engaged, serious threats were made. They considered David undesirable because he was a Christian and because he had the same last name. Although Chen was a very common name and the families could have been connected over 500 years ago, non-believers were very superstitious.

Normally, missionaries did not visit smaller cities but Yushin's mother had a small room that she consented to let a missionary use as a chapel. Neighbors came to learn about Jesus. When some men relatives found out about this, they threatened to break David's legs, hurt Yushin's mother or kill Yushin if they ever caught her. Yushin was not afraid, she ran from the city school to visit her mother in the country and back, and they never caught her. She was bold and not afraid of danger.

In 1934 when David was 26 and Yushin 20, he offered to call off the engagement because of the many threats. Miss Dodds said that Yushin would be safe on the compound and if there was a problem her mother could stay with her. Yushin's father was deceased. The couple remained engaged, Yushin continued in school, and she was a believer when she graduated.

6

The Jesus Chapel

The Presbyterian missionaries sent David to Tienhu to serve as a pastor of a small, country church, the Presbyterian Mission Church. It was in the center of town and the local people referred to it as the Jesus Chapel. From a pole on the top of the Chapel flew a flag that was visible for a great distance. A large cross and the message, "Believe on the Lord and be Saved!" extended an invitation for all to come to the Chapel and worship. Many answered this call.

These country people were not educated and did not know about the gospel. Even though he was not ordained, God blessed David's ministry and there were many conversions and healings. During this time David and Yushin corresponded and their affection deepened as their wedding date grew closer.

In 1936 he returned to Tengxian. Since Yushin had no dowry, David bought beautiful silk cloth and had a tailor make the wedding garments. Yushin's special wedding dress was a print fabric that featured delicate flowers. Her long black hair was coiled on the back of her head bringing emphasis to her dark eyes and delicate features. She made a beautiful bride. There was no veil because David could not afford one, but no one seemed to notice. David was dressed in a blue, silk gown. A Christian wedding was performed by Presbyterian Pastor Wu in the living room of the professors' home. Oscar Walton, other professors, and students attended the wedding.

After the ceremony, as customary the happy couple went to see their families. First, they visited Yushin's mother then David's father and sister. They could not afford a wedding trip.

David and Yushin returned to Tienhu to continue the work at the Jesus Chapel. Many people were sick with tuberculosis, some were demon possessed, and others worshiped animals as gods. Some possessed people were quite violent until the demons left, then they became calm and became Christians. Also, living just outside of town, there were some ferocious naked people. Often a friend or relative would drag them to the Chapel. David prayed to God and asked Him to grant them peace. They would awake and become recognizably human. You could talk to them. They would dress and come to Chapel.

In the Chapel some people were healed and became Christians. David remembers the many healings, especially one old gentleman, who had headaches all the time. He came to pray and David prayed over him. He stayed in the Chapel for several days at different times. Eventually, he was completely healed, and the headaches were gone.

Many people came from a great distance to get to the Chapel. When people stayed for several days, Yushin prepared meals for them. David praised God for all who were helped by his ministry God blessed his ministry and word of his success spread.

7

Anglin's Invitation

The Presbyterian church transferred David to teach at a school for girls. While he was there, he got a letter from Anglin asking about his life and ministry. David wrote to Anglin and told him why he left the Home of Onesiphorus in a hurry, his time at the seminary, his ministry and the healings at the Jesus Chapel. Anglin sent David a letter discussing the possibility of his coming to the United States to give testimony of Anglins' work at Onesiphorus. David was an example of a child whose life was dramatically changed by his time at the Home, and because he had worked in the office he could confirm how well the donations were spent. David was certain that his typing skills, helping with the books, and learning some English had opened another opportunity for him.

He left the school, and he and his wife went to the Home of Onesiphorus in Taian. Since his wife would stay behind to teach school and to attend the same seminary he had, he took her to Tengxian. She did not have many options, because her relatives were against their marriage, and she could not go home. Also, Anglin had only invited David, and realizing the tremendous expense, David never asked him if he could bring his wife.

For the next several months David remained in Taian and prepared for the big trip. Anglin interviewed him and told him what to prepare. Anglin also helped him obtain his passport and visa. For his physical exam David went to Jinan [Tsinan], where the Presbyterians had a university and hospital.

Originally, they were scheduled to sail from Qingdao [Tsingtao], off the coast of the Shandong province, but because the Japanese began an occupation of major coastal cities, they had to take a small coastal boat to Hong Kong.

When David's papers were reviewed in Hong Kong, the ship's doctor denied him boarding because of his eyes. He had what best can be determined as trachoma, which had been treated and healed many years earlier. Anglin told a pastor to take care of David, and he and the others went on to the United States.

After the ship sailed, the pastor placed David at a YMCA. David felt very alone. He was use to eating wheat and spoke only Mandarin. He had trouble digesting the hard steamed rice they served and could not speak Cantonese. Unable to eat or communicate, he cried and prayed. "Why do you leave me here?" he argued with God. Eventually the missionary took him home, and he was glad to eat some American food.

The Pastor took David to the port's British doctor and showed him a paper where the ship's doctor had denied David a boarding pass because of an eye problem. He also showed him a paper David had from the university hospital; where a Chinese eye doctor, a specialist from the United States, said that his eyes were okay. They were told that this document was not valid in Hong Kong because the doctor was educated in the United States not England. Political red tape was about to sabotage David's journey to the USA. Searching among his travel papers, David found an old paper from Taian, where a British doctor wrote a few lines saying his eyes were healed and he had signed it. Normally, it needed to be a formal printed document, but it was accepted because the doctor was British. Allowed passage by the port doctor, he left on the next sailing. David thanked God for the miracle of finding the old papers and their acceptance.

8

To the USA

In 1937, Mr. and Mrs. Anglin sailed to Vancouver, British Columbia, on the "Empress of Japan." They went on to Chicago where Mrs. Anglin rested from a previous illness. David followed the same route. He sailed on the "Empress of Canada" on the fourteen-day journey. Traveling in 3rd class, he had a stateroom in the bottom of the ship with the other Chinese passengers. It was a big change from country life. He had never been on a ship or even a large boat. He looked at the immense ocean and marveled at God's creation. After Japan, the boat hit open waters, and there was a bad storm. David and many other passengers were seasick, but in spite of this he had a good time on the ship. The sights and sounds were unlike anything he had ever experienced. The food was American-Chinese. Since the ship had originated in the Philippines, it was laden with fruit. David tasted his first banana and his first grapefruit. To him this was truly the Garden of Eden he had read about in his Bible. He played deck games and walked around the deck. There were some Cantonese Chinese on board, and he communicated with them by writing. He was amazed to see them gambling so casually with US money which was so valuable in China. They were laundrymen who had worked day and night to earn money. They were returning to the United States from a visit with their families. At this time, only Chinese men came to the USA. They were mostly employed in laundry work.

The ship docked in Vancouver and the snow was deeper than David had ever seen. He did not spend much time there but transferred to a smaller ship and went on to Seattle. When he arrived in December of 1937, David was twenty-nine years old and spoke very little English.

In Seattle, Anglin arranged for him to be met by a pastor who put David on a Pullman to Chicago. He watched the beautiful scenery in the mostly, undeveloped countryside. As the train crossed different mountain ranges, he stared in wide-eyed admiration at the beautiful mountains covered with snow. He was also impressed by the many windmills used for irrigation in the rural farm areas.

David spent most of the trip standing by the door, in between the train cars, watching the scenery. He does not remember much about the food or the stops. He was too excited with all the new sights. In all, he spent three days on the train, too excited to do much sleeping. This journey gave David confidence that he could travel alone with limited English. In Chicago, he was reunited with Anglin and his friend, Samuel Hsiao, another boy raised at the Home. Samuel and David were about the same age. Samuel was married and had a six-year-old daughter, May Lee. From the station, they all went to stay at a home for itinerant missionaries. David and Samuel shared a room, and Mr. and Mrs. Anglin took care of May Lee, who considered them her grandparents.

9

Touring with the Anglins

Anglin had brought all three of them to the United States so that David and Samuel could give their testimonies and May Lee could entertain by singing songs in Chinese and English. David toured with the Anglins, Samuel and May Lee. He gave his testimony in Chicago and other parts of Illinois, Wisconsin, Michigan, Ohio, New York, Florida, and Georgia. There was also a stop in South Carolina where Mrs. Anglin visited the orphanage where she was raised.

Mr. Lundmark was the US director of the work and he assisted Anglin while he was in the mission field. He had visited Taian in 1931 and could give a favorable account of the activities. He would go on ahead and book churches. Lundmark contacted the pastors about the program and coordinated the dates for each trip. A well-renowned businessman, he was the advance man for these two or three week trips.

Since no one in the Anglin party could drive, they traveled with a car and chauffeur, carrying a large amount of equipment with them. They put on programs, usually in the evenings, spending a day or two at each place, sometimes more. Different families took them into their homes so they did not have to pay for lodging. The schedule was designed to attract large gatherings and raise funds for the Home of Onesiphorus.

They rented a projector to show a special film on the Home. It was taken by Mr. Albison, a world traveler and big supporter from Minneapolis. At this time, this was quite a treat for the audience. This sixteen millimeter, silent film was about a half hour in length and was narrated by Mr. or Mrs. Anglin. The many scenes showed the boys and girls coming out of the compound, playing games, eating, studying, working, the girls' sewing, and so on. After the film, Anglin gave a message. Then, Samuel or David told what it was like to be a destitute orphan and have the opportunity to avoid starvation, become a Christian, get an education and learn a trade. They all wore Chinese clothes during the presentation. May Lee would sing songs in Chinese and English and make hand gestures. Then, the meeting was turned over to the pastor of the church, who would take an offering for their benefit. Afterwards, they gave away literature and books about the Home. They also sold homemade needlework, napkins, tablecloths, scarfs and other items that were made by the girls. In addition, they took orders for stacking tables made by the boys.

In October of 1938 the Home of Onesiphorus had a large convention at the Chicago Moody Church to cele-brate the 22nd Anniversary of the work in Taian and the 10th Anniversary of the Chicago office. By this time over 1,000 boys and girls had graduated from the Home. However, it was not a happy time for the Anglins, because the letters they received from China described the de-struction that was taking place as Japanese armies and airplanes moved from the coast to the inland regions. They learned that bombs landed near the Home, and there was some damage, but no one was hurt. The Anglins could only pray to God that He would keep their children safe.

In spite of wars in Europe and Asia and growing world-wide political unrest, the fund-raising tours continued into 1940. It was essential that they raise as much money as possible because famine and political uprisings constantly created bigger needs and more mouths to feed.

10

D.L. Moody — Man of Vision

Dwight L. Moody was born in 1837 in Northfield, Massachusetts. When he was only a child his father died suddenly. A month later his mother gave birth to twins. Betsy Moody was left with nothing but many debts and nine children under thirteen. Her husband's creditors walked off with almost everything, including the wood she used to heat her home. In spite of this, she was resolved to keep her family together. A pastor befriended her, pointed her to God, and baptized her and her children. Among other fine qualities she instilled in her children was a duty to God and others.

Moody had hopes and dreams of material success but only four years of formal schooling limited his options. He left the rural area of Northfield and took a train to Boston. An uncle hired him as a shoe salesman, and after three months, he was the leading salesman in the store. As part of his employment agreement he regularly attended church and Sunday school. He was befriended by his Sunday school teacher who taught him about salvation. His teacher visited him at the shoe store where Moody accepted Jesus as his Savior. Eventually, he had a disagreement with his uncle and left his employment. Since his church did not share his evangelistic zeal, there was nothing to hold him in Boston. He traveled to Chicago with two desires, to earn $100,000 and to talk to people about Jesus.

Chicago was a friendlier place. He worked hard for various employers, traveling on business all over the state but returning by Saturday night so he could be in Sunday school and church. Active in his church, he soon could afford four pews which he filled with an odd assortment of visitors and guests. As his personal financial situation grew stronger, he often sent money to his mother and others.

In 1856, Chicago was experiencing revival and Moody was deeply impacted by two people. Mother Phillips taught him the importance of prayer, Bible study and memorization of Scripture. Also, she was very involved in Sunday school work with street children, and she encouraged him to work in this field. He also received encouragement from J.B. Stillson who taught him how to study each book of the Bible in a more systematic way.

Moody saw a need to rescue impoverished children from the most horrible living conditions imaginable. He would go into the worst section of the slums, which the police called "Little Hell," and talk to the children about Jesus. Later, he rented a saloon, cleaned it up and had Sunday evening meetings. Moody would ride around the slums on a pony often bribing children with maple sugar or pennies so they would attend these classes. While others thought this was a publicity stunt, he was only interested in more children learning about Jesus.

He developed an unusual way to hold the attention of these mostly illiterate children. First, he gave short five-minute talks. Then, there was free time for them to be rowdy. Finally, there were songs and music to calm their spirits. This magic formula was repeated over about a two-hour period. The children sensed the love at these meetings and the attendance grew to over 300. With donations they built North Market Hall to accommodate the growing numbers, and the Sunday school moved to its new quarters. John V. Farwell, a devout Christian businessman, paid for the furniture and now the children no longer had to sit on the floor. In addition to monetary assistance, Farwell also helped Moody by making the upper echelon of Chicago available to him and by teaching him the social graces that he would need in soc ty.

Moody's success was largely due to his own lack of education. The children could relate to him. His fame spread and he was asked to speak at other schools. By the end of 1860, Sunday school attendance had reached 1,500. Abraham Lincoln visited Moody after the election. He told these poor children that he had also come from a similar background and by working hard and by putting into practice the lessons their teachers taught them, they too might become President of the United States.

Dwight met his future wife, Emma Revell, when he spoke to her Sunday school assembly about his ministry with underprivileged children. Emma was six and one-half years younger than he. Born in London, England, she was educated and would later supplement his education with tutoring.

Among his projects, Moody was instrumental in the creation of the YMCA (Young Men's Christian Association). He lived at the YMCA and they sponsored Moody's North Market Hall where he continued as unofficial pastor. The choice to commit to full-time Christian work came gradually over a four-year period. He was encouraged by Farwell who vowed that he would always supply Moody with the necessities of life. Also, Emma promised her love to him. She was now seventeen and had been teaching in his Sunday school and dispensing charity at the YMCA which had women as auxiliary members.

Moody's disadvantages became his strengths. God had given him many tutors, and he continued to question other pastors he encountered about the meaning of various Bible verses. His knowledge was constantly growing.

During the Civil War, he recruited 150 clergy and lay-people to help him set up tents for each regiment which were supplied with Bible literature and writing paper for letters home. He traveled to various cities holding up to ten gospel meetings a day for the troops. Thousands of soldiers were converted. Many later died in battle. In one unusual moment in history, he even preached to 9,000 rebel prisoners of war. It was during 1862 that he quietly married Emma, and she sometimes visited the battlefields with him.

The Sunday school continued to grow. So his street kids would have a place in which they would feel comfortable to worship, he started the Illinois Street Church, which was an independent evangelical church. All strangers were welcomed and, unlike other churches, the seats were free.

Moody had the opportunity to visit England and he made a big impact. He was invited to preach in many places. He made many friends among Britain's evangelical leaders.

After he returned to Chicago, donations were raised for Farwell Hall, a large multipurpose YMCA building which would be the first of its kind. In addition, John Farwell supplied a fully-furnished, new home for Moody and his family. A short time later, both structures burned to the ground. Immediately, fund-raising was begun and eventually a new building was built to replace Farwell Hall.

One evening in October of 1871, Moody finished preaching just as the fire bells rang out. Fleeing flames thirty feet high, he hurried home to his family. His two children were sent away with friends, while he and his wife stayed behind to help others. High winds caused the fire to spread quickly. To Moody, it seemed like Judgement Day. The worst fire in the history of Chicago destroyed everything near and dear to him. The Illinois Street Church, the second Farwell Hall (YMCA) and their second gift house on State Street were reduced to ashes.

Moody was invited to move to New York but he recognized that every need of others was not a call by God and he prayed for guidance. Because there were no funds to bring his family with him, he took a brief trip to England for Bible study and retreat. Always considering new opportunities, he made arrangements to buy Christian tracts from Dublin for paper costs alone. They were later placed in racks all over Chicago.

11

Training Others — MBI

From programs pioneered in England, he began his next challenging project. He sought to establish a training program for women missionaries. He wanted them to have the opportunities for education that were available to men in seminaries. Initially called "Mr. Moody's Theological Seminary," it consisted of a group of deaconesses under teacher, Emma Dryer.

In 1873, with all barriers burned away by the Chicago fire, Moody and his family went to England for two years. Singer, Ira Sankey, and his wife joined them. Revival followed them everywhere they went and enormous crowds turned out in Scotland, Ireland and especially London. Moody was not an orator. He emphasized God's love not his judgment. Speaking plainly in words that the common man could understand, the people loved and understood his simple message.

Before returning to New York as a world re-nowned figure, Moody led a successful fund drive and a YMCA was built in Liverpool, England. To avoid all appearances of their personally profiting from the work, Moody and Sankey refused any offerings for their expenses or ministry. Instead, invitational committees secured private funding for each of their trips. Sankey hymn books were printed at this time. This venture was so successful that over $35,000 in royalties were accumulated. It was finally decided to use the $35,000 to build a new structure for the Chicago Avenue Church that had been devastated by fire.

Back in the United States, meetings continued in Brooklyn, Philadelphia, Chicago and other major cities. Then Moody returned to Northfield, he spent several years establishing the Northfield Seminary for Young Women, Mount Hermon School for Young Men, and a summer conference program held at Northfield.

Emma Dryer continued with the outreach to women missionaries and waited many years for Moody to promote this work. Although originally for women, this work later included men. When adequate funds were obtained in 1889, the Chicago Evangelization Society opened. Later, it was called the Moody Bible Institute. It was designed to train men and women as pastor's assistants, missionaries, Sunday school workers, evangelists and for other fields of Christian service, both here and abroad. R. A. Torrey was the Superintendent from 1889-1908. He was a learned scholar and a graduate from both Yale University and Yale's Divinity School. He and Moody agreed that in addition to academic courses, the primary emphasis was to teach personal work, prayer, evangelism, missions, music and the ability of the Scriptures to transform souls and lives. By 1894, an evening school was established. A unique feature of all the Moody schools was that tuition was free so no one would be denied a Christian education. A hundred years after its founding, the Moody Bible Institute remains tuition free.

Mr. Moody (not "Reverend Moody") had no interest in the subtle differences between various sects. He advocated ordained and lay-persons to work together in a non-sectarian way. He was driven, ambitious and involved in Sunday school work, mass evangelism, personal work, education of workers and published materials for all these categories.

For him, Christianity alone did not ensure eternal life. What really mattered was a personal relationship with Jesus and the desire to follow Him and not choose to go one's own way. Moody had the ability to capture an individual's attention and bring him into a closeness to Jesus. This was the effect of the power of God working through him. He devoted his life to evangelism and revival. During his life he touched millions and after his death in 1899, his vision made possible many works including the various schools he started to train others to continue his work.

After Moody's death, R. A. Torrey, then James M. Gray, then Will Houghton led the Moody Bible Institute. On December 3, 1934, one month after the inauguration of Houghton, John and Betty Stam, MBI graduates, were martyred in China. This incident shocked the Christian world. The Stams were China Inland Missionaries and part of the few MBI graduates who paid the ultimate sacrifice for their beliefs.

During his presidency Houghton used his talents in promotion and declared a two-year celebration that would include two main events. The first was February 5, 1937 the Centennial Celebration of Moody's Birth Date. The second was Sunday, February 7, 1937 the Fiftieth Anniversary of the Institute or Moody Day which was celebrated in every state and thirty foreign countries. During this period, articles about Moody and his life were in secular and Christian newspapers and magazines. Also, rallies and conferences about Moody were held from New York to London.

A student newspaper was started in 1935, cap and gowns became part of graduation ceremony a year later, and then in 1938, they issued the first yearbook. Also in

1938, a new twelve-story administration building was completed at the Institute.

WMBI, Moody's radio station, had been on the air for several years but it finally got assigned a frequency of its own when the FCC (Federal Communications Commission) was established in 1934. By 1941, it was broadcasting all day.

Houghton saw Irwin A. Moon, a creative minister, present his "sermons from science" and he invited him to come to Moody. Later F. Alton Everest, a former professor from Oregon State University, joined Moon. Their first film, "The God of Creation," got rave reviews from the secular as well as the Christian community. The time lapse photography portrayed creation in great detail. These films received awards in both the scientific and photographic worlds and became a far-reaching ministry for Moody Bible Institute.

MBI was an exciting place to be and a degree from the Moody Bible Institute opened many doors for those who attended.

12

David at Moody

In 1940, David went to a graduation ceremony at Moody Bible Institute. It was a cap and gown ceremony and he was impressed. At this time he was not aware of the school's reputation for excellence. He spoke with Andrew Yang, a graduating student, who told him he could study and work his way through. Since a person who was educated in the United States could get a good job in China, David wanted to study English and Bible courses before returning home. Although he wanted to stay, he did not know how he would be able to support himself. Tuition was free but he would have to earn his room and board.

Andrew introduced David to Professor McCune who had been a missionary to Korea. He was fond of oriental students and was acquainted with the wife of Mr. Crowell, Jr., Vice President of Moody. Mrs. Crowell had wanted to be a missionary but never had the opportunity.

David spoke to Anglin and told him of his desire to stay in Chicago and go to Moody Bible Institute. Initially Anglin was against the idea, because he had sponsored him and wanted him to return to China. David explained that he had spent three years in the United States and he would like an education at MBI which would help him get a good job in China. Anglin said he could stay if he could find someone to release Anglin from his responsibility with immigration. Professor McCune signed a release and became David's new sponsor.

Now, David was praying to God, "How will I pay for this?" Meanwhile, Professor McCune told Mrs. Crowell about David. She met David and told him that he would not be able to support himself right away because he did not know the language. She offered to pay about $90 for the room and board for his first semester, about three months. Others paid for the rest of the year.

The first semester was very difficult because of his limited knowledge of English. There were no textbooks and the students were expected to take notes from the lectures. Fortunately, David received some assistance from his fellow students who allowed him to review their notes. After the first year, his English improved significantly, he needed less help and he found it much easier to complete his class work.

He started working at the beginning of his first summer and continued during the rest of his time at MBI. It was a big school and David and many other young men did janitorial work, mopping floors in the classrooms and kitchen. Later, he worked in the kitchen washing dishes, pots and pans. He was paid $.30 to $.40 an hour for his efforts.

On Sunday mornings, David listened to the preaching of Dr. Ironside, Pastor of Moody Church. In the afternoon, he taught Sunday School at a Chinese church in Chinatown. His pupils were mostly laundrymen who were trying to learn English. In addition, he joined China prayer bands with other students who were interested in missions.

In July, 1940, when the Anglins returned to China with Samuel Hsiao and his daughter, they had to deal with the Sino-Chinese War and the thousands of starving people fleeing from the Japanese. China was not equipped to fight. The missions were forced to move inland. Many missionaries were forced to leave but the Anglins remained. When the bombers came, the children would all drop to the ground and pray until the bombs stopped. Although this was an almost daily occurrence, no child at the Home was ever hurt. Meanwhile, in a nearby village, 700 persons were killed in one air raid! Over time, the Japanese were able to destroy, kill, and burn most of the property.

On December 7, 1941, the Japanese bombed Pearl Harbor. The next day the United States Congress declared war on Japan and all Americans were advised to evacuate; but, again, the Anglins refused to abandon their family. Later the Japanese struck against Clark Field, USA's principal base in the Philippines, and overran the island. Eventually, Chinese communications with the rest of the world were cut off and Japanese troops attacked American properties in China. Asia was in chaos and on February 5, 1942, Singapore fell to the Japanese. This was the biggest military disaster in the history of Britain. The Japanese had seized control of the Pacific and committed many atrocities.

After Pearl Harbor, the Lundmarks ran the Chicago office for two years without any official word from the Anglins. When news did come, it was bad news. Rev. Anglin's health declined as he dealt with the stress of the Japanese and the devastation he saw everywhere. In September of 1942, Rev. Anglin died of meningitis. David visited Mr. Lundmark at the Chicago office to keep up on the news of the Anglins and the Home. After Anglin's death, Lundmark took over and ran things from the United States.

Shortly after her husband's death, the Japanese took over the Home and placed Mrs. Anglin in a concentration camp. The Japanese sent her and other missionaries to a camp in another city, where she spent twenty-nine difficult months. With little food, all of them had to eat worms and rice to survive. During her absence, senior boys ran the Home. After the war in 1946, she and others were repatriated. Before returning to the United States, she opened another children's home in Jinan. When she finally returned to the USA, she rested and wrote articles for *The Harvester*, until her death in 1952.

13

Delayed by World War II

David completed the two-year course at Moody Bible Institute in four years. He graduated in 1944 and was ready to return to China but could not because of WWII. He stayed on at Moody until 1946 working as an elevator operator and doing kitchen work.

Since his arrival in the United States, David wrote to his wife as often as possible. Retreating from the Japanese troops, the mission school where she was teaching moved inland and to the west. From city to city, they fled–walking during the night, sleeping during the day–and always on the alert for planes. There were constant air raids. The young male students carried the bedding and supplies. Yushin Chen fled with her students. She comforted the younger ones, encouraged the older ones and constantly prayed that someday she would be reunited with her husband. After Pearl Harbor, there was no mail as the Chinese Government also had to retreat. Within the compound of her school, the US flag protected her and her students. The final stand of the government and the mission was in Chongqing where Mr. Horace Williams was a missionary and interpreter for the US Army.

Mr. Williams came on furlough to the New Tribes Mission in Chicago. One day Williams rode an elevator at Moody Bible Institute where David was the operator. The American talked to David in Chinese and David asked him where he came from. When he replied Chongqing, David told him his wife, Yushin, was there. Williams told David he knew Yushin and told him where she had been evacuated. Williams was acquainted with the school where she was teaching. Before he left China, Yushin had asked Williams to contact her husband. For three years there had been no communication between the couple, and they did not know if the other was dead or alive. In 1945, after Japan surrendered and mail resumed, David was finally able to write to his wife. She remained in Chongqing with her school until after the war.

In 1946, in a desperate attempt to bring his wife to the United States, he transferred $1,000 of his earnings to China through a merchant. She received it but it became worthless overnight because of currency problems. It was not enough money to bribe officials for a passport and buy a ticket for a trip to the USA.

In 1946 Mr. Paul Fleming started the New Tribes Mission in Chicago. David worked for them using US Army books to teach Chinese to missionaries that were planning on going abroad. Originally, David had expected to return to China as a New Tribes missionary. He applied, was accepted, and expected to be joined by others after he arrived in Shanghai. Two other students went to Hong Kong then to Canton, meanwhile things changed drastically, and they were unable to go to Shanghai. New Tribes intended to send missionaries to the interior of China but their missionaries were forced to withdraw to Hong Kong, Japan and other places. New Tribes was never established in China because of war conditions, and David had to find another job.

Pictorial

Home of Onesiphorus Tailoring Department – Chapter 3

A

Touring with the Anglins – Chapter 9

Back: Samuel Hsiao & David Chen
Front: Leslie Anglin, May Lee Hsiao & Ava Anglin

B

David, Mr. Hedberg & Rev. Stralnic – Chapter 20

C

Dwight L. Moody,
founder
Moody Bible Institute
Chapters 10 & 11

David's graduation
from Moody 1944
Chapters 12 & 13

David Chen and wife, Yushin 1980 – Chapter 20

Yushin Chen, Rev. Finley & David 1984 – Chapter 20

Toni and Harvey Milkon – Chapter 21

Chaplain Wyeth Willard
Chapter 23

Willard Family – Chapter 23 – Back: Leah, Bethany & husband, David Willkinson, Rachael & husband, Rick Toothaker, Wyeth & Wendy Willard. Front: Jean & Peter Willard

David Chen
Chapter 25

David Chen & Toni Milkon

Phyllis Milkon
& David Chen

Chapter 26

K

14

Return to Shanghai

David spent ten years in the United States. He toured with the Home of Onesiphorus for three years, spent four years studying at Moody, then worked until WWII ended and he was finally able to return home. During this time, he remained a Chinese citizen with a Chinese passport. In April of 1947, he sailed to Shanghai on a warship that was temporarily being used for passenger travel. He paid his passage from the money he had earned at New Tribes and Moody. Before he left, he wired both his wife, Yushin, and his sister, Ruilan, that he had obtained definite passage. Yushin was in Chongqing when she received the news, and she made arrangements to return to Shanghai.

As his ship sailed into the Shanghai harbor, his family anxiously awaited his arrival. When the ship docked, David was on an upper deck looking for them through his binoculars. He was overjoyed to see his wife, and his sister and her family. To get their attention, he started throwing candy on the wharf. Although some went through the planks, the excited children were able to get a few pieces and they enjoyed the exceedingly rare treat. David went to the baggage area to go through customs. Since there were many people, it took all day. The customs agents reviewed his smaller pieces, and they took many of his things, some as simple as a comb or notebooks. Although he was upset, he did not dare complain. When he finished, he went to where his family was waiting. Even though he had not seen his wife in ten years, there was no public display of emotion for, at that time, this was unheard of. In their thoughts, David and Yushin thanked God for sparing their lives and reuniting them again.

They left in a taxi and went to Ruilan's home. He and his wife lived at his sister's home for about two years. After the war, his brother-in-law, Ernest Yang, as an officer of the Chinese Army, had first privilege to live in one of the nice homes evacuated by a Japanese family. Unfortunately, shortly after their arrival Ernest was taken away by the Communists, imprisoned, then assigned to a hard labor camp.

When David arrived in China, General Chiang Kaishek was in power. The economy was terrible and currency devaluations were frequent. In Shanghai, he was forced to convert his US money to Chinese. Later, when he returned for his large baggage, he paid customs duty with a bag full of folded money! Because of corruption and huge debts, the government paid their bills by printing more money. This led to runaway inflation. Currency became worthless and eventually people were throwing it away.

Although David was glad to be back with his family, he was unprepared for the conditions he found. He thought a returning student from the United States would get a good job. Instead, he found confusion. The country was on a precarious footing with financial devaluation, few remaining old, social customs, and moral decline instead of law and order. There were many thieves. One day, while he was riding in a street car, someone stole his Parker pen. He was surprised, but found out that fountain pens were considered very valuable. David was constantly shocked by the contrast between the China he had left, the United States where he had spent the last ten years, and the reality of the world in which he found himself. Originally, he thought he would get a good job and start a church. As it became obvious that nothing of that kind was going to happen, his expectations vanished.

During WWII, China and the United States were allies against Japan. After the war the IRO (International Refugee Organization) had leftovers from the US Army which were distributed to churches, welfare organizations, hospitals, orphanages, etc. David's knowledge of both Chinese and English allowed him to get a job with the IRO. He was hired as a manager, worked with a Chinese staff and was fortunate to be paid in US dollars.

By 1949, mainland China had been taken over by the Communist Party. Chairman Mao Zedong proclaimed the establishment of the People's Republic of China and General Chiang Kaishek evacuated to Taiwan.

15

CNEC — Fred Savage

CNEC, which became Partners International in 1985, was formed by many people with special talents. God prepared and brought together a compassionate missionary from Northern Ireland, a committed couple from England, a dynamic lay-leader in Seattle, a gifted Chinese evangelist in China, and many others.

Duncan McRoberts, a missionary from Northern Ireland, while he was living in a village in North China, saw how effective the "native Chinese" evangelists were in introducing their countrymen to God. In addition to helping the evangelists, Duncan was courting Winnie Savage. Her parents, Fred and Geraldine Savage, of England, were living in Shanghai and working for a commercial company. Since they were self-supporting, they could pass on support funds from overseas to the Chinese.

Calvin Chao was a well-renowned Chinese evangelist. He and many others were forced westward by the invading Japanese Army. Duncan McRoberts and Winnie, now his wife, were also forced to leave. Her parents were not as fortunate and were placed into an internment camp near Shanghai. When Duncan McRoberts and his wife came to the United States in 1942, their reports on the conditions in China moved many people, including Cephas Ramquist who later became a board member. He put McRoberts in touch with Dr. N. A. Jepson of Seattle, Washington, who had helped to found an organization for Christian businessmen known simply as CBMC.

Jepson responded to the challenge of helping the native Chinese reach their people because he already believed in this idea. He called together several men who, in God's plan, were all in Seattle on business at that time. They met with Duncan McRoberts and founded the mission known as "China Native Evangelistic Crusade" (CNEC). They sent a cablegram to China asking Calvin Chao to prayerfully consider leading this ministry.

Chao considered this God's answer to prayer because he and his co-workers had been in the mountains praying to God for the resources to evangelize their countrymen. Duncan McRoberts was employed as field director. The board was comprised of Jepson, as President, and many prominent businessmen from California, Washington and New York. Their diverse backgrounds and experience helped to establish a unity of purpose. Since they assumed all the financial obligations, in the early days all funds received were sent to the mission field. The mission expanded into China and later to Hong Kong, Thailand, Singapore and other places.

Eventually, Mr. Fred Savage took over the finances from Calvin Chao. This arrangement worked out well because Mr. Savage was a British businessman. As the work expanded beyond the mainland of China, the name was changed to "Chinese Native Evangelistic Crusade." An International Coordination Office for CNEC was established in Hong Kong and Fred Savage took care of the administration. Savage had lived in China for 40 years and had helped many nationals with his own money. Funds were channeled from the supporting countries through the Hong Kong office to the various fields of ministry.

During this time, Professor Chang was Principal of Taitung Seminary. Chang, like David, had graduated from the North China Theological Seminary and then he had gone to Princeton University in the United States. Professor Chang heard that David had come back from the USA and that he was a Moody Bible Institute graduate. Professor Chang took a trip to Shanghai and visited David. He asked David, "Do you want to serve God?" David said, "Yes." Chang offered him a job. David and his wife went to the Taitung Seminary in Nanjing where he taught general classes in the Bible and helped with the business accounts for the seminary until it was evacuated.

When the seminary was relocated because of the Communists, David and his wife returned to Shanghai. David obtained a job at the CNEC office working with Fred Savage. He helped with the books, administration, and money exchange. Political conditions deteriorated and in 1948, the British government forced their citizens to evacuate to Hong Kong which was a free colony under British control. As a British citizen, Savage left Shanghai in a hurry. Savage's wife, Geraldine and their children had departed previously. Thinking this was only a temporary situation and that he would be returning soon, he did not take many of his things. Before he left, Savage asked David to take care of his home, furniture and belongings.

Savage's home was foreign and considered very modern by Chinese standards. Although there was no refrigerator, it did have a gas stove, fireplace, flush toilet, bath tub and wood floors. It was very unusual to have a tub because most people went to the public bath house. Also, the wood floors were a vast improvement over the normal dirt or brick floors.

David was Secretary of CNEC and he, along with Miss Chen (no relation) and Mr. Wang, acted as a committee of three to handle the work of the whole mission. David was in charge of correspondence and the transfer of money. As the money was devaluated, there came a point where he had to estimate its value based on how many units of rice, cloth or coal it could buy. Also, there was rationing of many items.

CNEC supported gospel bands. These were groups of local Chinese evangelists that usually came from a home base to spread the gospel. This continued after Savage left. Now, Savage sent funds from the United States via Hong Kong to David in Shanghai.

16

A Moment of Joy

After David returned from the United States, his wife's first pregnancy ended in a miscarriage, but their disappointment was replaced by joy when she became pregnant again.

When Yushin went into labor on September 23, 1950, the hospital had not been fully taken over by the Communists and was still operating as a private hospital. Ultimately, Yushin needed a Caesarian but before her doctor could operate he had a heart attack. Mrs. Liang, an employee of the hospital and one of their distant relatives, got another doctor to perform the operation and deliver the baby. During this time, David had been watching the birth of his first child and taking moving pictures. His wife was under the anesthesia and was not aware of what was happening.

The baby had been overcome by the anesthesia. The doctor held the lifeless form in his hands and announced, "The baby is dead." When David heard this he was stunned. He put down the camera and did not know what to do. Immediately, the doctor tried to save the child. He gave the baby oxygen and she was revived. After a spank, the baby cried and David rejoiced and praised God for saving their child. They took the baby away to wash her and put her in an incubator. Because of this difficult delivery Yushin was unable to have any more children. Yushin was hospitalized for one week, then she and David returned to the Savage home in Shanghai where they were currently living.

David named his daughter Meien, in English this means "beautiful grace." At the time of her birth, David was 42 years old and Yushin 36. As new parents they were overjoyed and planned the announcement of her birth in the customary Chinese way. When the baby was one month old friends, relatives, Christians, pastors and associates were invited to their home. David and Yushin had a large basket of eggs that were colored red (for a girl). They passed out the eggs, received baby gifts then entertained everyone with a big dinner. David was so happy that he could afford this luxury.

17

Hitting Bottom

In the 1950's the Religious Bureau of the People's Republic of China chose to control all religions. The Three Self Patriotic Movement [self-supporting, self-governing and self-propagating] began. Later, the TSPM were the official open churches. At that time, these churches required the acceptance of government rules. Also, there were many "do's and don't's" regarding religious practice. In addition, the underground, or house churches, started.

On February 8, 1951, David sent a letter from Shanghai to Mr. and Mrs. Lundmark (Home of Onesiphorus, Chicago). He explained that since the beginning of the year, all churches, institutions and religious bodies had to register with the government and that they were not allowed to receive any foreign funds. He explained that everyone was afraid to correspond with anyone from abroad and that even persons receiving mail from the coastal cities of China were suspected of reactionary activities. David cautioned them not to write nor send any funds to the children's homes in Taian or Jinan. Furthermore, he stated that he and others were looking for jobs beside Christian work because, according to the government, it was imperative that all must work. Also, he informed them the government may take over all private institutions. With a brief note mentioning they were enjoying their five-month-old baby, he ended asking only for their prayers. There was a great sadness in the

Chicago office when they read this letter. By the end of 1951, all Westerners had to leave China.

From 1950 to 1956 David was self-employed. With no secular work available for Chinese mission workers, he often did mission work for free.

The Savage home was rented from a land company. The government took away the title because of back taxes which no one could afford. Now the property was owned by the Chinese Government. David got a notice to pay rent to a house land company which was a department of the government. He was upset about the amount because he could not afford the payments. Meanwhile the tenants formed a committee to protest and they received some rent reductions. He still could not afford the total amount for the house so it was divided. His family used the second floor, bath, kitchen and one bedroom and he rented the first and third floors to an evangelistic Bible lady. She used the first floor as a chapel and lived on the third. Sometimes David preached. Before the lady was arrested, she rented the third floor to another lady. Eventually, six families were housed in this house, with one family per room.

David was working with the house churches which were unregistered. To maintain a living and support his family, he sold his possessions since American things from abroad were a novelty for the Chinese. For a while, he also managed with the US dollars he had earned but by 1953, he had used the last of his US funds. With a three-year-old daughter to support, he tried to get a job. It was very hard because the economy was so bad, and he had no training in the business world. He started a small business in his home manufacturing soy milk and delivering it to his customers. His wife helped him. They even hired a girl to take of the baby while they were working. He also taught typing lessons. Things were not going well. David had to tell the gospel bands that there was no money from abroad and that they had to support themselves. They disbanded and returned to their trades.

A critical year for David was 1958. With all his resources exhausted, he was forced to ask the government for a job. First, they put him through six to eight months of indoctrination to convert him to the beliefs of the new society. Then, he got a job at a cooperative doing heavy work. During this time, teachers and other intellectuals were seeking manual jobs.

Times were very strange. Although a person was free to express his opinions, if the government thought he was thinking in the old way, he would be branded a rightist. They expected everyone to be a revolutionary. The consequences for being a rightist were severe. The individual lost his job and was denied ration coupons.

Most people were employed in cooperatives. It was a way of running things. It was run by people who made many things and shared in the labor and profits. Later, cooperatives were made into big factories which were State operated with a party member in charge. David was assigned to work in a lumber yard. His days consisted of carrying, peeling and cutting logs. It was heavy work which was generally given to the "bad element." With no safety equipment, many workers became ill. David eventually became sick from breathing the sawdust. He developed high blood pressure and heart trouble.

David and his countrymen were experiencing the consequences of the policies of Chairman Mao Zedong. Mao organized the "Great Leap Forward" to increase crop production. He forced agricultural collectivization of the

63

farms under some peasants and used others to produce steel. This effort to solve shortages and problems ultimately created turmoil, misery, and famine. Mismanagement by the bureaucrats caused millions of Chinese to die from famine.

In the mid 1960's, there was a new kind of proletarian-led movement called the Cultural Revolution. It called for students to rebel against authority. Once it started, things rapidly got out of control. By 1966, radical Maoist students, known as Red Guards, brought revolution to China. When their activities turned to anarchy, Chairman Mao Zedong had to turn to the military to regain control.

18

Unwelcomed Visitors

David and his family lived on a quiet lane. Each home on this lane had a separate entrance gate that was usually locked. One night someone deliberately left his gate open.

At 3:00 a.m., a noisy pounding on their door woke everyone up. A loud voice yelled instructions, "You have to get dressed." It was a hot evening toward the end of August in 1966. Red Guards, so called because of the red bands around their arms, stormed in and took control of David's home. Some were classmates of his sixteen-year-old daughter and knew that the family was Christian.

David, Yushin and Grace were separated so they would be unable to talk to each other. Each was guarded by different guards and subjected to relentless questioning. Guards watched them twenty-four hours a day even while they were sleeping. After three days they had some communication with each other as the search and interrogation continued.

The Red Guards thoroughly searched their home for weapons, counter-revolutionary articles, secret radios and other items. They dug holes in the yard, made holes in the walls, and pried up floor boards looking for proof of crimes, American money or treasure. They went through all their belongings, clothing and personal possessions.

One boy, thinking they had hidden money in the chimney, climbed the roof and came down the chimney covered with soot. David thought he looked like the devil and he felt anger growing within him. He trembled with rage because he wanted to hit this boy but God intervened and stopped him. The red arm band gave any boy the authority to go into any house. If David had resisted him in the slightest way, he and his family would have been put to death.

Money was never found but they seized a small amount of jewelry, a penknife, watches from the USA and all credentials including their marriage certificate, his Social Security card and his passport. They also looked in a trunk where David had stored several typewriters because he sometimes taught typing for a living. They thought these were instruments that could be used to communicate with a foreign government. Knowing the actual use of these items, it did not occur to David that their findings were of much importance. In addition, they found two small American flags he had put in the trunk and forgotten about. All of these items were locked and sealed for later investigation.

The Red Guards told David that he hated the new China and loved the United States. Placing hats on their heads and placards on their chests, which proclaimed David and his wife "foreign agents," they forced them to stand on a temporary platform in the street. David tried to pull his daughter to the platform but the Red Guards said no. Grace was separated from her parents and taken to the side. She was told that she had been adopted by these American spies. Grace was terrified. She had heard that this type of thing had happened to other families but never thought it would happen to hers. An anti-revolutionary sign with huge characters was hung on their gate with glue. David and his wife were paraded through the lane so all their neighbors could see their disgrace; then they were taken back to their home.

The Red Guards had been told to do something for Chairman Mao Zedong and they had accomplished their goal. These unwelcomed visitors remained in the Chens' home for about one week. Then, during the following week they escorted David to and from the factory where he continued to work for the next two years. It was a difficult time for him and his family because they were totally isolated from the outside world. They could not send or receive any mail and any public phone call was monitored. Everywhere they went they were followed. Since any person they talked to would have been suspected they did not even dare to say hello to anyone. David and his wife were branded "bad elements." Their daughter was told her parents were anti-revolutionary. They called her parents "dogs" and she was a "puppy child."

One month after the Red Guard visit, older men came to the Chens' home and opened everything again. These labor workers carefully checked the radio for secret messages from the United States. Finally they hauled away all the household goods and the trunks on a big truck. Everything went first to a church then later to a warehouse where it was stored. Now, the Chens had to sleep on the wood floor. They, however, did not complain because usually floors were only dirt. Food was scarce and they lived mainly on porridge made of rice and vegetables. That same year Grace finished high school but she could not go to college because her father was classified a criminal.

In some ways the Chens were more fortunate than others whose dwellings had been so ripped apart that they were not livable. Also, their faith sustained them and spared their lives. Other neighbors were so distraught that some committed suicide after their homes were ransacked and family members were taken to prison.

The Cultural Revolution continued over a ten-year period and during these times, confusion and destruction reigned. Homes were ransacked, businesses were disrupted, schools were closed, transportation was interrupted and tales of rampages were commonplace. Nothing old or Western was exempt from destruction and everything from artwork to Christian books and Buddhist relics were burned in the street.

The Red Guard continued to impose impossible regulations. They would measure the width of your trouser leg. If it was narrower than the measuring string, the wearer was subjected to taunts, violence and punishment for bourgeois dress. Strange rules were enforced. Red was considered a good color and green was bad. This caused some accidents at traffic lights because confused drivers did not know whether to stop or go on red. The Cultural Revolution destroyed anything that appeared to be foreign. There were killings, riots, battles on the street and brutality between the different factions.

19

Valley of the Shadow

One day in 1968, a party member who ran the factory where David worked told him he could not go home. He was detained and placed under guard where he assumed he would remain for one night. David asked permission to telephone his wife to tell her he was not coming home but his request was denied. All the other workers left while David remained there alone with a few guards. He vividly recalled the horror of his first night in the factory. A light bulb burned all night to deliberately torment him and sawdust smoldered creating heavy smoke which made it difficult to breathe. It was a hot summer night and David was choking. Desperate for air and thinking he would suffocate, he jumped out a main floor window. The guards caught him and interrogated him the rest of the night.

Meanwhile, his wife and daughter waited for him until late that night. His abrupt disappearance was disturbing but there was nothing they could do about it. As days turned into weeks, their anxiety increased. Finally, someone came to their home and told them to send clothes to David. His family made up a small package of the items he had requested–a toothbrush, clothing for winter, bedding, etc. David was under house arrest. Because he had spent time in the United States, they considered him an American spy.

The dormitories in the factory where he had been detained had just a bed and a window. At first, he was alone but later he shared a cell in a damp cellar with another man. It was impossible to sleep at night because of the mosquitos. The other fellow went crazy and screamed slogans from Mao Zedong's red book all through the night. The guards beat him to shut him up but he wouldn't stop. Sometimes the guards would beat both of them. They thought they would get credit for treating their prisoners harshly, so they did this to please their superiors and Chairman Mao.

Cruelty did not stop with the guards. Other abuse occurred. With his hands tied behind his back, David would be forced to kneel on the floor or a narrow bench while party members took turns interrogating him. In the beginning, they also whipped him during these sessions. Each time the whip struck his back, David winced in pain as he struggled to maintain his balance. He knew that if his body or head moved or if he fell he would be beaten even more severely. One day after a few strokes of the whip, David fell. As the beating intensified, the pain became unbearable. Silently, he prayed to God, "What am I going to do, I can't take it any more." After his cry for help, God honored his prayer and the pain stopped while the beating continued. Later he remembered, ". . . My grace is sufficient for you . . ." 2 Cor. 12:9

Beginning a few weeks after his confinement, they held struggle meetings two or three times a week at the factory. Later, they were held at least once a week. Struggle meetings were held in front of the workers as part of their education. They used David as an example of what would happen to them if they did anything against their country. During these meetings, they used slogans such as: "Down with Chen, the anti-revolutionary!" Often, he was slapped in the face. Also, other workers from the factory attended these meetings and they beat him, spit on him, humiliated him, kicked him, and hit him, too.

In order to find out what crimes someone committed against China, they demanded to know every misdeed he could remember from the time he was six years old. Each day, David was required to write everything down in complete detail. He wrote many, many sheets. He was continually writing confessions and turning in a few pages every day. The committee that reviewed this information was impossible to please.

After many struggle meetings, David had a dream that someone poked him in his stomach with a big stick. As he woke up screaming, God gave him a warning not to give away the name of other missionaries or evangelists because he would make trouble for them. When David did name names he only gave the names of those not at risk, such as people that had evacuated or were deceased. He told them that Mr. Savage had asked him to take care of his home and household goods. The more information he gave them the more they demanded. When he did write, he used the longest words he could think of and repeated a lot. They did not believe the truth.

One working-class guard wore high boots. He came into David's cell for no reason except to show his girl friend the authority he had over the prisoners. As he proceeded to kick David from one corner of his cell to another, his horrified girl friend ran away.

On another occasion, David was hiding behind the door to his cell and praying on his knees. He had overlooked the window above his head that was guarded twenty-four hours a day, seven days a week by guards on the outside. One particularly sadistic guard passed by, looked through the window and saw him on his knees.

"What are you doing?" he demanded to know. "I have a stomachache," David responded. "No, you are praying and you have to confess." After his first denial, David finally admitted he had been praying. "Tell us what you are praying for?" he commanded. For this minor infraction, David was beaten severely; then, for additional punishment, he was forced to kneel on a jagged piece of iron. As the jagged metal tore into his bleeding flesh, he was pushed to the limits of his sanity. He never forgot this time of agony.

Afterwards, David was given a sheet of paper to put down what he was praying, who he was praying to, and why he was praying. He completed one sheet of paper after another. Although they tried very hard, they could not exhaust him into admitting he was an American spy. The pile of sheets grew to an inch in height but David never admitted to being a spy.

After this incident, David wrote the story of the prodigal son because he felt he was not worthy to be God's son or servant because he had initially denied that he had been praying. David felt he had betrayed God by not being bold in his beliefs. The guards delivered the story to their supervisors and David assumed that someone probably read it.

They constantly accused David of many things including that he had taken pictures of factories and airports. Many times they said that other people had told them things he had done. David decided to write down whatever they said to try to avoid the beatings but nothing seemed to help.

During each struggle meeting, David would be brought in as a prisoner. They would ask him to describe his crimes against China. After his response, they would say they did not believe him and would often slap him anyway. This cycle of frustration caused some Chinese believers to renounce their faith and turn others in to save themselves.

David and other religious and political prisoners that would not renounce their faith were separated and transferred from the factories to the riverfront in Shanghai. There were many pastors from different churches. Here David was confined in a small cell in the cellar of a big warehouse where he lived in solitary confinement. These were very difficult times.

At the factory and at the riverfront, David read Chairman Mao Zedong's red book and his poems because they were the only ones permitted. In addition to reading he was continually forced to write. Once David used Mao's book to lean on while he was writing on a sheet of paper and for this he was severely rebuked. Defiling this book could result in death. A hot water tender at the factory used old newspapers to stoke a stove. When he realized that Mao's picture was in the paper he destroyed, he jumped into the river and committed suicide because he feared they might kill him when they found out.

David was accused of being an American spy because of the "evidence" they found from the search of his home. This included the two American flags, a long kitchen knife, which they thought must be a weapon from the USA because China had nothing like it, and especially the typewriters, which they were convinced were telegraphs to send messages to the USA. Ultimately, they wanted David to confess to his crimes.

During his time in prison, David was put through every indignity imaginable. As his psychological pain increased, he became a tormented soul. He contemplated suicide as the only way out of the severe beatings and a situation which, after years of cruelty, he viewed as totally hopeless. One Sunday all the workers were gone and David found himself alone with only two guards. First, he placed the gold bridge for his teeth that he had made in the USA in his pocket then he wrote a note on waste paper, "I'll see you in the next world." One guard came and sat next to him telling him to write. "Write, write!" he thought. "Life is not worth living." Defeat and desperation seized him. David saw there were hammers and screwdrivers on the desk where he was sitting and he thought of killing the guards to escape but God told him they were not to blame and were just doing their job.

David thought of ways to end his life. He could run out of the front gate to the busy street and be killed by passing cars. This idea was abandoned as there was a guard watching him every minute. He thought he could go to the back gate, climb up the stairs to the top floor and jump off to be killed instantly. Food came but he did not eat it. His mind was on a desperate plan to end his suffering. Finally, an opportunity came. One guard went to make rounds. David told the remaining guard he needed paper. Alone, he took this brief moment to run to the back gate and up the steps from the first to the second floor. He thought it was a five story building but there were no more steps and no other escape. David had run madly to avoid the guard that was chasing him. Determined to take his life, he looked out a window and saw what he thought were waves and this encouraged him to jump. He threw himself out of the window, landed on the concrete and fell on his side. He injured his foot and arm and was bleeding all over. Although badly hurt, he did not sustain life-threatening injuries and had no broken bones. The guard had called for help to catch him and soldiers came and took David to the police station. The city police had no jurisdiction because David was a resident of another district. As David sat in a pool of blood, a medical person sewed him up. The police had to decide what to do with him. They called party members while David sat there in shock, fearing nothing. Temporarily they decided to lock him up in a smaller place with wires above the bars. It was a storehouse without a window and had a small cot. But first, they gave him a harsh whipping because, by attempting suicide, he tried to blame them for the crime of persecuting David Chen.

When David jumped, he broke a woman's washtub and board. He would have to pay for them. While he was in jail, he was allowed to send his monthly salary of about $30 home to his family. Now, this expense would come out of the money he sent them. During his imprisonment, David was required to buy food tickets for each month. This also came out of his pay. Toward the end, one sympathetic guard allowed David to buy a plate of meat with a ticket. Food was very limited. Prisoners received about three ounces of rice and a small bowl of cooked vegetables per meal. This was hardly enough to sustain a grown man.

After spending time in the smaller place, David was eventually taken back to the factory.

20

Tears of Joy

Periodically Grace went to the factory to inquire about her father but the answer was always the same, "We don't know." They would never tell her where he was or when he was coming home. Eventually, his daughter found out that he had been moved but they still could not tell her where. One day, when she asked about her father, a woman party leader said to her, "You say God blesses you. Why doesn't He come down to deliver you?"

Since her husband's imprisonment, Yushin found herself without enough money to live on. They tried to force her out of her home but she would not leave. Tenaciously she said, "If we are going to die, we are going to die here."

Yushin had to go to indoctrination classes because everyone had to be re-educated. Later, she got a job working in a local residence association which consisted of several families. Residence associations employed mostly women, the handicapped or invalids that couldn't work in the factories. People were organized for collective living to do things and to contribute to the group. Yushin did not have a choice about the type of work she must do. She was assigned to mend clothes and repair rubber shoes. She worked until she became very ill from the fumes of the charcoal stoves that heated the unventilated room where she worked.

In 1968, Grace was eighteen years old. All children had to undergo re-education, especially children whose parents were accused of being "bad elements." Normally she would have been required to go to one of the re-education farms on the China Russia border; but she never went because her stubborn mother would not send her. Instead, she had some re-education in the neighborhood two or three times a week.

Grace and a boy named Tsengwoo were assigned to do hard, dirty, manual labor. They had to feed the furnace for a steel mill with coal or wood. They did not know about each other's families but became friendly over time. Because of the danger of confiding in the wrong person, people did not discuss their personal lives. At that time, Tsengwoo's family was also having problems with the Cultural Revolution. Although they considered themselves Chinese, his father was Japanese and his mother was Chinese. When it was discovered his father was of Japanese descent, he was put under house arrest. Later, he was jailed because they thought he was a Japanese spy. The family had been well-to-do before all their goods were taken away. Tsengwoo was one of six children born in Shanghai. After his father was jailed, the children were separated from their parents and raised by an aunt. When his father got out of jail, he went to Japan and eventually earned enough money to send for his wife and children.

By 1971, China was looking for diplomatic ties with the rest of the world. United States Secretary of State, Henry Kissenger's talks with Chinese Premier Chou Enlai, resulted in President Nixon's historic visit in 1972. Prison attitudes were changing and questionings and torture abated to some degree.

One night in 1972, Grace prayed to God, "Please bless my father and let him come home." Later that evening, a call came that they were to come and get him. At one of the official gatherings, it was decided to let David go. His daughter came to the factory to pick him up. After a separation of four long years, David and Grace cried tears of joy when they saw each other. David was released from the factory and the party was now freed from any responsibility for him because a family member had picked him up. When they were leaving, David told his daughter to bow to the pictures of Chairman Mao, the superintendent of the factory and other party members to thank them. Then, they returned home where Yushin was waiting expectantly. The night of his release was the first opportunity David had to talk to his wife and daughter since his imprisonment. They stayed up all night while he told them what he had gone through during the years they had been separated. Although David was free, he was under surveillance. After about six months, he was finally allowed to go to and from the factory alone.

David was the first one from his factory to be jailed, the only one that tried to commit suicide and the last one to be let out. After his release, David recalled the verse that sustained him, "Even though I walk through the valley of the shadow of death, I will fear no evil, for you are with me; your rod and your staff, they comfort me." Psa. 23:4

One of the guards savagely kicked and beat his prisoners including David. Through many beatings, David never asked God for vengeance. One year after David's release he saw a man with a bandaged hand walking toward him. God spoke to David and said, "I saw all the beatings he gave you and he will never beat anyone again." Later, David found out that this guard had lost his fingers in a sawmill accident. Another tormentor was the boss over the guards who constantly encouraged everyone to beat David. When this boss was opening a barrel with a blow torch, the fumes caused an explosion that seriously injured his leg. He became lame. In both cases, God's vengeance was severe.

David worked at the factory from 1972 to 1975. His work was lighter now and more skillful but the pay was the same. He carried logs and sawed wood and then made jewelry boxes. His wife had the same job mending clothes and shoes. Grace continued to do manual work and taught some private English lessons in childrens' homes.

Grace visited Tsengwoo and his family in Japan in 1973. The following year, he came to China and married her. Pastor Liu performed the ceremony in the home of his daughter. Afterwards Tsengwoo took Grace to their home in Japan.

In 1975 David retired at 67 years of age. A year later, Savage died without realizing his dream of returning to his home in Shanghai. That same year Chairman Mao Zedong died and the members of the Gang of Four were denounced and put on public trial. The four were accused of trying to seize power after Mao's death. Ironically, one of the four was Mao's widow. The radical leftists were discredited, economic growth was stressed and universities were reopened. Later Deng Xiaoping, a moderate, emerged as the leader of China. In 1979, China and the United States resumed diplomatic relations and a US embassy was established in Beijing.

During this time house churches were holding meetings in different homes. David participated by letting them use his home. Meanwhile, in Japan, Grace gave birth to her first child, a baby girl. David and Yushin were delighted to be grandparents.

As travel restrictions were modified, David was visited by friends. Mr. George Hedberg, the current president of the Home of Onesiphorus, and Rev. Gus Stralnic visited Hong Kong in 1980 and took a short trip to Canton-the farthest they could go without visas. Their destination was the Canton Trade Fair and the Chinese Government had just okayed travel by small parties. They went by hovercraft up the Pearl River and stayed at a local hotel. One of the boys, Hon-Lun, a graduate from the Hong Kong Children's Home, was pastoring a church in Macau. He came to Canton for this meeting. At this early juncture, ordinary Chinese citizens could not travel within China without police permission. David came down from Shanghai on the train to meet them. Also, ordinary citizens could not enter the hotel unless they were brought in by a hotel guest. Hon-Lun brought David to the hotel and Stralnic went outside to greet both of them and bring them inside. Although he had previously talked with David on the phone, this was their first face-to-face visit. After dinner in the hotel dining room, Stralnic and Hedberg took David to their hotel room and gave him some Chinese Bibles and a couple of warm, winter jackets. The next day they visited the Evangelical Free Church Bible School of Canton, known as the Canton Bible Institute, and the local Bible women. It was an inspiring visit for all and later David returned to Shanghai.

On another occasion, Rev. Allen Finley, President of CNEC, his wife, Ruth and Paul Chang went to Shanghai to visit David. [CNEC was currently known as Christian Nationals Evangelism Commission.] The Chinese Government controlled where they went and where they stayed. Since they would give no advance notice of the tour schedule, it made it difficult to meet someone. The

CNEC office was able to get a message to David regarding their arrival date. At the last moment the tour took an earlier train. Upon their arrival they were taken to their hotel and told to rest. Chang and Finley smiled when they realized that the hotel was within three blocks of CNEC's headquarters (Savage's home). Leaving Ruth behind to deal with any inquiries by the tour operator, Chang and Finley left the hotel and quickly walked over to CNEC. When they arrived David was eating lunch and preparing to meet the afternoon train. Their reunion was enjoyable but brief because of the danger to David and his family as well as themselves.

Grace called the public phone on the lane and someone contacted her father. He spoke to her and was delighted to find out that she and her one-year-old daughter would be coming for a visit. There were no private phones and a call from Japan was considered a big event. While Grace visited her mother, classmates and friends, David enjoyed taking his grandbaby to the park close to his home.

21

Precious Cargo

When their ship docked in Shanghai, Harvey Milkon, an American tourist, had to push his wife off the ship in a wheelchair. A few days earlier, she had broken her ankle in Beijing. When he saw the buses, he began to make arrangements for a car and driver. The China Travel Bureau [the official government travel bureau] had other plans. They insisted that he and his wife travel by bus for the tour. Harvey refused to be coerced by the Communist guards. He gave them a hard time and insisted on a private car arguing successfully that his wife couldn't manage on a bus. After much wrangling, the guards agreed to a car and driver.

The ship's passengers disembarked and proceeded to the gate where buses were waiting to take them on a sightseeing tour of the city. They could not see the Chinese citizens at the far end of the shipyard because the buses were lined up and faced a stone wall. Harvey helped his wife, Toni, into the car which was on the opposite side where there was an open view of the surroundings. In the distance, Toni saw a Chinese man who was holding up a sign. She thought he was the doctor with whom they had been corresponding and were expecting to meet for the first time. Harvey walked down to the man holding the sign. He was ready to greet Dr. Zhang [not his real name].

David Chen stood in the crowd with a small sign saying "Milkon"; he was overwhelmed by the noise and confusion coming from all these foreigners. Then, a tall man introduced himself as Harvey Milkon and accompanied David and his young companion back to the car. Neither was aware that Chinese citizens were not allowed within three blocks of the dock. When they arrived at the car, David greeted Mrs. Milkon, "God is with you." Surprised, Toni asked, "How do you know?" "Someone has written to me telling me to meet your ship," he said. "You have on board what our home church has been praying for." With those words, Toni knew that David had been sent by God and that her prayer, to bring Bibles to those who were praying for them, had been answered. "I was going to bring another older man with me today," he continued "but at the last minute, I chose a younger man. God knew you needed help." Then, he introduced himself as David Chen, a Chinese evangelist.

Upset by his wife's broken ankle and focused on taking care of her, Harvey had almost abandoned the plan of delivering Bibles. After this event, he began to see the magnitude of God's plan. There were very few Bibles in China and David's house church had been praying for a long time. Later, when this first encounter was reviewed in detail by all parties, no one was able to determine who told David Chen to meet the ship. Someone sent him a letter to meet the "China Explorer" in Shanghai on a specific date and gave him the name "Milkon." He didn't know who the Milkons were, where they came from or what they were bringing with them.

With Toni sitting safely in the car, Harvey decided to return to the ship. Meanwhile, Toni talked to David and his friend, Wayne, who were standing outside the car. Harvey returned to their stateroom, opened a suitcase, and unpacked 150 pounds of Christian books. When they were in Beijing, they purchased two huge duffel bags with Chinese characters. He transferred the precious cargo to these bags. Balancing one on each shoulder, he success-fully maneuvered the bags through the ship's narrow corridors, down the gangplank and the long walk to the car. This was an extraordinary feat for a sixty-five-year-old man with back problems. During this entire time, David, Wayne and Toni prayed that the Communist officials would not be aware of what was happening. Toni knew Harvey was getting the books but she did not know how. The duffel bags were not part of the original plan.

The guards saw Toni, the wheelchair and the crutches and the two Chinese men. This acted as a complete diversion from the real mission. Toni's heart pounded as Harvey approached the car. He quickly placed the duffel bags in the trunk, added the wheelchair and crutches and shut the lid.

Originally, they were supposed to follow the tour buses. As Harvey got into the car, he told the driver that he was taking the two men with him. He did not give him an opportunity to protest. The men got into the car and they were off to visit a Buddhist shrine. On the way, Toni showed David Chen Dr. Zhang's address and asked if he knew where it was. He said it was close to his home. At that point, they decided to skip the tour and do God's work. Harvey gave the driver the new address and they went directly to David's home. When they arrived, the men carried the books up to David's home while his wife, Yushin, came down to the car to greet Toni. She did not speak English well and was very timid but she was cordial and smiled with the knowledge of the precious cargo. Harvey and David hid every book. David was overwhelmed by the Bibles, gospels, dictionaries, concordances and

Christian literature that tumbled out of the bags. Bibles were so scarce that some people painstakingly copied one chapter at a time and shared them. The Bibles David received were very precious because no amount of money could buy one.

Toni explained to them that she had written to many missionary organizations about bringing Bibles to China. All of them had told her that it was far too dangerous. As the weeks before her 1983 departure date dwindled, Toni was surprised to find books of every kind arriving on her doorstep. This large assortment of Christian literature was never ordered and never paid for since it came from sources unknown. The books were in Chinese or bilingual. Also, due to an airline error, the suitcase containing the precious cargo and the Milkons and their other luggage were routed on to different planes from Florida to California. Then, in God's perfect timing, the precious cargo made its connection from California to Hawaii then on to Japan where they boarded the ship.

The next stop was the home of Dr. Zhang. David spoke to the doctor's wife and found out that he could not meet the ship because he had to work that morning. She asked them to come back for tea. They agreed to return later and caught up with the tour to avoid suspicion.

Later, they returned to Dr. Zhang's home, a four-floor walk up. The younger man whom David chose at the last moment, provided the necessary manpower. He carried Toni up the stairs on his back. It was moon festival time and they were served almond cakes with egg inside and tea with unstrained tea leaves. Toni found that Dr. Zhang had received some of the medical and bridge books she had sent previously. With David acting as interpreter, the gospel message was shared. The Zhangs were extremely grateful for the visit which ended with the customary exchange of gifts. The Milkons received a Chinese tea set and gave the Zhangs a unique, calendar pen. They said goodbye and had to return to the ship.

On the return trip, David informed Toni that she ad no idea what she had done. In the Chinese mind she had suffered great indignities for her God by allowing herself, cast and all, to be carried up to see them piggyback style. He told her that this was very rare occurrence and that they would never forget what she had gone through to talk with them.

Harvey suggested that David, Yushin, Wayne and his girlfriend join them the following day for the next stop on the tour. He said he would get a station wagon and they would go to the lake in the Wuxi area, a famous tourist resort. David explained that there was no such thing as a station wagon. Harvey said, "If God has brought us this far and if there is a station wagon in China, God will find it!"

The next morning at 7 a.m. the four of them showed up with a station wagon and driver that Wayne was able to get. On the way to the lake, Toni asked David to tell her the true picture of the church in China. She explained that she had heard conflicting reports in the United States. Needless to say, he whispered the whole way so the driver would not overhear what he was saying. He spoke about his daughter, Grace, who also suffered for her faith. He was glad her prayers sustained her but he was disappointed it was not safe to teach her more.

After arriving at the lake, Toni and Harvey offered their banquet tickets to their four guests. They were going to buy something else for themselves. The Milkons found out that this was not allowed. Finally, their guests were permitted to order some rice but they had to give up their rice rations tickets. Toni and Harvey were able to slip them a few items, but they were dismayed by the limitations imposed by the Chinese government.

It was time for the driver to return them to the ship. Harvey told David to tell the driver to take them to their homes and that he would pay any additional expense. David explained that the driver would not be allowed to do it. It was late at night and they all had to take buses home.

Sometime after their return home, the Milkons found out that during their visit to China an anti-crime campaign was in force. In Shanghai alone over 11,000 persons were jailed for various reasons including having superstitious materials like Christian literature. It was not until then that they realized the full danger of the mission. Looking back on her accident, Toni Milkon remembered that while walking alone and praying she felt an unexplainable force knock her face down to the ground. At the time, she thought that something supernatural had happened but did not know why. Now, she realized why her ankle was broken, not sprained as she originally thought. God had used her broken ankle to enable her to have a wheelchair, car and driver to accomplish their mission. They praised God for his protection from prison or worse and thanked Him for their new friend, David Chen. David thanked God for their courage in risking their personal safety to bring the precious cargo for his church. For the next two years, the Milkons and David corresponded with each other. They were only allowed to exchange limited information because the mail was subject to censorship.

22

A Visit Abroad

Mrs. Hall was a travel agent from Portland, Oregon, who took tourists on trips to China. In 1984, she was contacted by a Christian organization [name withheld] and asked to find a speaker for their program in Japan. They wanted someone who could discuss the status of believers in China. On her next visit to Shanghai, she visited Pastor Wang Ming Tao who told her about David Chen. She contacted David and asked him if he would speak at a Christian seminar in Tokyo. Coincidentally, David was trying to obtain visas to Japan so he and his wife could visit their daughter and grandchild.

David wrote to Toni Milkon for advice. He explained that two missionary organizations had contacted him asking him to speak in Japan about his experiences in China. Because of the delicate nature of the stories, he asked her which one he could trust to protect him and his family from the press. He did not want to put his family in jeopardy. At this time, China was very strict and did not allow churches, missionaries or Bibles. He knew severe punishment would result if word of this got back to China. Toni suggested an organization that she and her husband knew.

David's original passport had been taken from him during the cultural revolution and his wife never had one. After a considerable amount of red tape, David and his wife applied for and received passports from the People's Republic of China. They also received visas from the

Japanese Consulate. They were only able to obtain the visas because they were going to visit their daughter.

In October of 1984, David and his wife left for Japan on a three-month visa which they renewed in Japan. They spent a total of six months in Japan and their second grandchild was born during their stay. His daughter rented an apartment near her home for them. David and Yushin spent this time enjoying their visit to Japan and their role as grandparents.

David made his first contact with the Christian organization in Tokyo. He and others spoke to the organization's Japanese leaders. He was the only Chinese speaker. David was glad to find out that there were so many Christians in Japan. He told the participants many stories about religious worship in China. They listened attentively while this humble man of God described some of the stories about his life. In their closed sessions, they learned the difficulties of believers in China.

Mr. George Hedberg was the past-president of the Home of Onesiphorus which became Kids Alive International in 1983. Hedberg was a friend of Canadian Pastor John Kao. Hedberg suggested that Kao visit David in Shanghai which he did and they became acquainted at that time. Later, when David wrote letters to Kids Alive in Chicago, Hedberg shared them with Kao. Pastor Kao was connected with Partners International in San Jose, California, and, when he found out David was in Japan, he told them.

Partners sent word to David and invited him and his wife to come to the United States to visit them and others. Meanwhile, the United States Consulate in Japan told him he must return to China and then apply for a visa. He knew he would never be able to get a visa from China to go to the United States. In a bizarre twist of fate, his old confiscated passport was returned to his home in Shanghai and his nephew forwarded it to him in Japan. When David was in Tokyo for his speaking engagement, he went to the American Embassy there. He met a lady official who had a missionary friend, in Nanjing, and she had learned some Chinese. She was sympathetic to David's predicament. At first she said no, but, when he showed her the old passport to prove he had been to the United States and that his visa had been extended many times, she reconsidered. She spoke to her supervisor and they agreed to issue visas for David and his wife to go to the USA.

In Japan, David contacted several persons. One was Dr. John Young, an American pastor. At an earlier time, Toni Milkon had written to him and asked him to contact David's daughter. David obtained his name and address from Toni and visited Young. During their visit, Young recalled that almost forty years earlier in Nanjing, David had lent him his motorbike for Young's evangelistic outreaches. David brought the motorbike with him on the ship when he returned from the USA but found that he could not afford to pay for the gasoline. They spent time discussing their current ministries.

On a Japanese peninsula, David visited two missionaries, Miss Jeannie Leiyn and Miss Hildagard Meyer from New Tribes Mission. Many years earlier, he had taught Chinese to one of them. Both had originally gone to China but had to withdraw to Japan because of political conditions. David was asked to speak to their large congregation. He spoke in English and they translated his words into Japanese. Their congregation was very enthusiastic about his message.

Several years before Mr. Browman visited David in Shanghai he stayed in his home and discussed with him the children's home that his father had established in Japan. When he was in Japan, David took the opportunity to visit these children's homes where foster parents cared for ten or twenty children in their home. He found the children clean, healthy and happy. On Sundays they all worshiped together. After Mr. Browman, Sr. learned that David was going to the United States, he helped him with his expenses and gave him the names of several friends including Peter Willard of Chop Point Camp in Maine.

In March of 1985, David and his wife left for the United States with visas that should have been issued in China. Partners helped by buying their round trip airline tickets and friends gave money for their expenses in the USA. Although they had no money for the trip, God had supplied all their needs. Because of a special that was running at that time, Korean Airlines gave them several free coupons that could be used for domestic travel between other cities.

The Chens arrived in San Jose, California, from Japan and stayed with the Finleys. Rev. Allen Finley was President of Partners International [formerly CNEC]. They were met at the airport by Mr. Chuck Wilson, Jr., Director of International Services. He helped them in various ways during their stay especially in arranging all their travel plans. The trip served as a vacation for them and they were able to thank all those who supported and prayed for them during those difficult years.

Yushin, who was suffering from exhaustion, stayed behind to rest. David went on to Chicago and visited different people he knew from his days at the Moody Bible Institute. Dr. George Sweeting, the current

President, asked David to give his testimony during the morning chapel hour. Later, he invited David for lunch with some of the faculty. David found remarkable changes since he had graduated in 1944.

Yushin was suffering from a serious case of asthma. Over the years, Toni Milkon wanted to send her medicine but David said the government would not allow it. The medicine in China had not been sufficient to help her and they had no medical insurance. The outing with the Milkons at the lake in China was the first time in a long while that she had been out of their apartment. During David's trip, her condition worsened. She was under a doctor's care and nursed by Mrs. Ruth Finley. Mrs. Finley took very good care of her and a bond developed between the two women. Yushin was very shy but she would talk to Ruth. When she realized that she did not have to be afraid if someone heard her speaking English, she relaxed. Then, her broken English improved dramatically and she started to recall words she learned in school. While she was recovering, Yushin often sang old Christian hymns in Chinese.

Upon David's return from Chicago to San Jose his wife was feeling better. He was invited to go to Chop Point Camp for the summer by the Director Peter Willard. He contacted Willard to discuss the arrangements.

23

Chop Point

Rev. Wyeth Willard chose to serve God instead of pursuing a career in business. In the late 1920's, he was offered 20 acres of land on Cape Cod for $500. He bought it, dedicated it to God and formed a non-profit Society For Christian Activity. On this property in 1935, he and his wife Grace established Camp Good News to win young people for Christ.

In 1942, during WWII, he decided to apply for a commission as a Navy Chaplain. Only after, he was convinced he would have the freedom to preach as he had done in the civilian world. He graduated fourth in his class and was the first Baptist chaplain to graduate. He was advised to make out his will before leaving because he might not be coming back.

While he was in San Diego waiting for the "President Adams" to sail, he was introduced to a member of the Gideon Society who offered him Bibles. Eventually all 2,400 were stored aboard. At sea, during a series of interviews, Chaplain Wyeth compiled a list of the 1,000 Marines with their name, rank, serial number and parents' names and addresses. Each Marine was given a Gideon Bible, some of which saved lives in unusual ways. During fierce battles on three different occasions, bullets tore the prayer books apart but saved the soldiers' lives. Another soldier bent over to retrieve his Bible and felt a bullet graze down his back making a burn instead of striking him in the stomach which would have happened if he had remained standing.

Willard was the sole survivor of the eight Navy Chaplains who landed with the Marines at Guadalcanal. The ship sailed on to New Zealand where he had an urge to buy a hatchet. As the urge became an order, he bought it. Later, he used it to make crosses over the temporary graves. (Many bodies were later removed and reinterred in the United States.) After the war, he resigned his commission as commander in the Navy Chaplain Corps.

Over the years, Rev. Willard purchased adjoining land and eventually had over 200 acres with one-half mile lakefront property. During his absence in the Pacific campaigns, his wife served as acting director of Camp Good News. This camp became three camps and they are currently run by their daughters, Hope and Faith. Annually, they are visited by 300 campers.

A second camp became a reality in 1966 when "Merrymeeting Camp" was available for sale. Renamed Chop Point, it is run by Rev. Wyeth Willard's son, Peter, his wife Jean and other family members. Chop Point consists of fifty acres on a beautiful, rural, wooded peninsula on Merrymeeting Bay in Woolwich, Maine. Campers come from across the United States and several foreign countries to enjoy good food and a wide range of athletic activities. Both camps encourage campers to study the claims of Jesus Christ in an interdenominational atmosphere but they are not pressured or manipulated concerning their spiritual beliefs. With a focus on changing hearts rather than on having ten thousand rules, kids see the attractiveness of Jesus in the lives of the staff and how this is available to everyone. Young people gain self-confidence and hope in a world which at times seems to lack hope. Also, they are inspired to choose worthy and unselfish goals.

The numerous success stories include campers whose Chop Point experience changed their lives forever. John was an honor student involved in the drug culture. He acknowledges the "good work" Jesus Christ began in his life in 1970 and credits Chop Point. John later graduated from a top medical school, completed a residency in neurosurgery and is happily married with a family. Trisha was a camper in 1978. Her initial reaction was "get me out of here" but by the third week she had prayed to receive Jesus Christ and her life was completely changed. For years, she worked for public relations firms, then she became the Director of Public Relations for the Bowery Mission, which serves the homeless and inner city children. Another camper named Bret, was one of ten children, Chop Point had a positive influence on his life and he went on to become the mayor of a large metropolitan city. The stories go on and on, each touching and heart warming.

David Chen decided to visit Chop Point. He and his wife flew from California to Chicago to New York, where he left his wife for a visit with his nephew, Paul Yang. David arrived at Chop Point and, during his visit, the Willards were impressed with David's sweet spirit and the campers enjoyed his company. Later on, Yushin and their grandniece, Fawn, joined him at the camp.

Toward the end of their visit, something aggravated Yushin's asthma; she became extremely ill and was hospitalized. David rode in the ambulance to the hospital. Peter Willard called Partners office in San Jose and found out that, fortunately, she was covered under their group policy. She had an allergic reaction to the drugs she was given; her condition worsened and she became delirious. She didn't recognize David who stayed with her day and night to interpret and help her. Peter sent some of the staff from Chop Point to help David so he could get a break. Jean recalls how patient David was with his wife.

At one point, Jean stayed with Yushin so David could get a little rest. Jean recounted how Yushin became distraught and attempted to pull out her IV's. Jean's calm reaction avoided a serious situation. To soothe her, Jean began to sing old Christian hymns. Yushin listened attentively then she started singing the hymn in Chinese. To the hospital staff, it was a strange sight to see two ladies praising God in two different languages but they were impressed when Yushin calmed down.

When Yushin was better, they flew to New York, dropped off Fawn then traveled on to Chicago where Yushin was to visit with her Chinese friends while David went on to Atlanta, Georgia.

24

Calls Around the USA

Mr. George Hedberg left his home in Rockford, Illinois, picked up David in Chicago and drove to Atlanta, Georgia. They were going to represent Kids Alive International for one week of meetings. On the way, David had a premonition that something was wrong but he never mentioned it to Hedberg. Meanwhile, Yushin Chen became critically ill and, much to the concern of everyone, she died at the home where she had been visiting. Telephones rang all over the United States as the news of her death spread.

Rev. Gus Stralnic from Kids Alive's headquarters in Valpariaso, Indiana, called George Hedberg in Atlanta to tell him that Yushin had died. Stralnic thought David should return immediately. Hedberg waited for evening to gently break the news to David. He told David that he could fly to Chicago or, if he preferred, he would drive him back. After much prayer and serious thought, David decided to stay in Atlanta. He made this decision because he had the peace of knowing his wife had gone home to be with her Savior. Also, there was nothing that could be done until their passports and visas were sent from San Jose to Chicago. A call was placed to Partners in San Jose notifying them of Yushin's death and requesting the necessary documents.

At this time, David was staying with a very caring family from the Riverside Church in Atlanta. He vividly remembers how this family reached out to him during this incredibly sad time in his life. They were extremely sympathetic and comforting and he never forgot their kindness. He spoke at the Riverside Church and told them stories of his years at the Home of Onesiphorus [currently Kids Alive International]. David touched the hearts of those who heard his message and these earthly angels reached out and comforted him.

David notified his grand nephew, Zhang Ming, who happened to be attending school in Chicago with his wife. He helped with the funeral arrangements. Zhang also contacted his mother in California who, in turn, called David's daughter in Japan.

After the meetings, David was driven back to Chicago by Hedberg, David did not know what to do because he had no money. Hedberg called funeral homes and got prices. Then he took David to the Hanorhoff-Hultgren Funeral Home in Wheaton, Illinois, because he was acquainted with Mr. Hultgren. This funeral home agreed to help them. The Hanorhoff-Hultgren Funeral Home went to the Chicago morgue with Yushin's passport, identified her, brought the body back and took care of all other arrangements. The burial service was attended by many guests and friends including the Consul General and Vice-Consul of the People's Republic of China who had to notify China of her death. David was grateful that the Lord provided such a beautiful burial service for his wife. After the service, he asked about the settlement of his account. He was told it was free of charge. A small insurance policy from Partners and financial help at the request of Mr. Vernon Hultgren took care of all the expenses. David was amazed since he had never experienced anything like this. He thanked God for this miracle and the earthly angels that made this possible. After the burial, he found two juniper trees and a headstone of polished granite that were placed over her grave. The simple inscription on the tombstone said "Beloved wife and mother Chen Yu-Xin (Mary V. Chen) born 1/21/15, died 8/7/85." [The modern spelling of Yu-Xin is Yushin.]

After the Chicago funeral, David returned to San Jose where a memorial service for his wife was held at the offices of Partners International. Ruth Finley spoke about Yushin's good nature, her good deeds and Christian character and mentioned memories from their recent time together. David was overwhelmed by the love and caring of the friends that took part in the service. Now, he was alone with no place to live. A family from San Mateo, California, Steve Overstreet, a representative for Far East Broadcasting Co., came to Partners. They had met David in China and invited him to stay with them. With the tragedy of his wife's death finally having an impact, David was glad to be able to visit friends. He was their guest for a few months.

25

Partners — Political Asylum

Toni and Harvey Milkon contacted David and asked him to visit them in Florida. Toni thought it was miraculous that he was in her home only two years after their visit to China. They spoke of many things, especially how Americans could help the churches in China.

After his Florida trip, David returned to San Jose, California, where he prayed and asked God whether he should stay in the United States or return to China. Meanwhile, Partners International received a warning from a Chinese evangelist saying that the authorities were going to David's home looking for him. He advised them to tell David not to return to Shanghai. A friend went into David's home and retrieved a few personal items of little value and sent them to his daughter in Japan.

This latest development was discussed by Rev. Allen Finley, President of Partners and Arthur Gee their East Asia Coordinator in Hong Kong. Gee had been informed that others had been questioned by the Chinese Government because of the information in one of David's letters. They decided it was too dangerous for David to return to China. Meanwhile, George Cover helped David find his first rental apartment in Palo Alto.

After he stopped traveling, Partners sponsored David and assisted him with his application for a green card. When the paperwork was complete he began working at their headquarters in San Jose. David shared a small office where he translated letters and did general office work. After he finished his work, he often volunteered to help those in other departments. He enjoyed being useful and everyone remembered his willingness to perform any task. David also assisted them in identifying pictures of the Chinese workers they had supported. David never had a driver's license but he was able to get to work by bus and, around town, by bicycle. In addition to his salary, he received support from his many friends across the USA.

Rev. Finley introduced David to the Crossroad Bible Church which had an outreach to the mostly Buddhist refugees from Cambodia and Vietnam. David's next calling was to tutor them in English and Chinese as well as explaining the gospel message. Like David, these people had also fled the Communists and their similar experiences created a common ground for helping and encouraging each other.

A tired man in his late seventies, David Chen was ultimately forced to seek political asylum in the United States. Rev. Finley found a Japanese attorney who was a Christian and sympathetic to David's plight. He assisted David with the necessary paperwork. Partners assumed financial responsibility and many other persons vouched for him. Rev. Finley accompanied David to immigration with his petition. At first, the State Department said there was no problem with China. This news was discouraging because everyone involved knew that David faced imprisonment or worse if he returned. Periodically, immigration was contacted to find out the status of his petition. Then, for about one year, they could not locate his paperwork. Partners was concerned because they had copies of the letters of recommendation and testimonials but not of the application itself. During this period,

David was uneasy and lived in fear of being deported. Finally, after several years, the US State Department approved his petition.

While attending Moody, David worked for about ten years. He discussed this with Harvey Milkon who told him he was probably eligible for Social Security benefits. David explained that when he was imprisoned in China all his records were destroyed. Harvey interceded for him and wrote to Washington, D.C. He obtained his Social Security number and found out that David qualified for benefits. With this good news David learned that once again God had supplied his needs and abundantly. In God's perfect timing, the additional years David spent working in the USA during WWII, enabled him to have financial support during the later years of his life. Also, how could he ever imagine that when he prayed for Bibles he would meet friends who would one day assist him in obtaining his Social Security benefits?

While David resided safely in the United States, years passed and human rights violations in China continued. In 1989, much to world-wide disbelief, tanks rolled into Tiananmen Square and the Chinese Army fired on protesters–killing unarmed people.

26

"Retired" in California

Ruilan, David's sister, spent her life in China but her daughter and son came to the United States. Her children sponsored her and she made a trip to California. David visited with the three of them. When she first arrived, he asked Ruilan questions about their childhood. They both had told others their mother had died but actually they never really knew what happened to her. Ruilan told him their father had remarried but she could not tell him any details about his childhood because they were separated at such a young age. After a short while, her memory failed and their talks ceased. She died in California.

Because he had a niece and grandnephew in Southern California, he eventually moved there. David obtained a studio apartment with a nice view in a church-sponsored building for seniors. He believed that he was blessed. One year David's daughter came from Japan to visit him and they flew to Chicago together so she could visit her mother's grave.

Throughout his life he never ran out of things to do. In his eighties David went to school to learn Spanish to help with his missionary outreaches near the Spanish communities. But he became discouraged and gave up the idea because the classes at the city college empha-sized grammar and writing, not conversation.

David was invited to visit Rev. Peter Cannon and his wife, Pat (Milkon) Cannon in Columbia, South Carolina. They run H.I.S. [hisinternational.org], a ministry that helps international students with their everyday needs and is available to answer their questions on Christianity. They were delighted to have David visit them and he stayed for about a week. During that time he spoke about the church in China to students at their ministry and at some of the local churches. He fascinated his audiences with his testimony and tales of his ministry and survival. The Cannons had a special party in their home in David's honor. One guest was Rev. Kepler who had been a missionary in China until he was forced to leave. Since Rev. Kepler and David were about the same age, they had many things to discuss and they enjoyed reminiscing in Chinese. They had heard of each other's ministry and thought they may have met when they were younger. David and the Cannons enjoyed their precious time together and David also became acquainted with some of their children.

On another trip in 1991 David visited Kids Alive for their 75th Anniversary. He spoke at banquets in Chicago, Minneapolis and Atlanta. When not traveling he was a guest of John Rock, President (now retired) and his wife, Louise. They became well acquainted with David during his three-week visit.

Back in California traveling by bus or bicycle, David attended services and functions at three different churches, one of which was Chinese. Also, when a pastor was absent, he was sometimes asked to give his testimony. Churches included him in many of their events. One church had a barbecue on a ranch outside of the city. Always an enthusiastic participant, David enjoyed the food and played all the games including volleyball, badminton and ping pong.

In August of 1997, I went to California with my mother, Toni Milkon, and met David Chen for the first time. We discussed the possibility of writing his story. In God's great plan, his daughter was visiting him with her children. Grace was able to supply information that David was not aware of, especially what she and her mother endured during his imprisonment. David learned how Grace prayed constantly for his release and had called out to God the night he was set free and her prayer was answered. David and Grace also shared other details for the first time because they came from a culture where people were used to suppressing their thoughts to avoid negative consequences. While I was conducting these initial interviews with David, there was news that China was cracking down on individual churches–especially those receiving outside funds.

Also during this time, Toni shared with Grace that she had been praying for her since her 1983 visit to China. Toni took advantage of this visit to explain to Grace why the gospel was so important and Grace's faith was strengthened.

In his nineties David slowed down, gave up his bicycle and rode the bus more often. After calling to congratulate him for his 90th birthday Toni Milkon became concerned when he did not answer his phone for several days. She thought something had happened to him. After several weeks he called to tell her that he had traveled to Canada alone to visit Russian friends that he met when they were passing through Shanghai many years ago.

Currently, David is never idle. When he is able, he volunteers his time at the local primary school where he helps with office work. Also, every Friday he divides large bags of donated beans and rice into smaller packages for a local food service agency that distributes groceries to the poor.

David has a special way of spending the holidays. He joins a Philippine couple and their eight children and takes a bus to the Salvation Army where he helps with the children and everyone enjoys a good dinner. David's only negative comment regarding these trips is the amount of food that is thrown away. After years of deprivation, it distresses him to see any food wasted.

In 1999 as he approaches his ninety-first birthday, he lives alone, does his own grocery shopping, cooks, takes care of his laundry and still finds time to reach out to others with letters and small gifts.

27

Conclusion

David Chen's life was dependent upon a host of earthly angels that established Christian works that directly benefited him. These persons heeded God's calling, persevered in accomplishing their tasks and served as God's messengers. In addition to those that started these endeavors, many persons devoted their lives so that they would continue.

When David sought refuge from deprivation and hunger, he went to the Home of Onesiphorus [now Kids Alive International]. If Rev. Leslie Anglin had not established this children's home, David probably would have starved to death as a young boy. Instead, he became a Christian, graduated, attended the North China Theological Seminary and later went on a fund-raising trip for the Home that gave him the opportunity to travel all over the United States.

In the late 1800's Dwight L. Moody founded what later became the Moody Bible Institute. David remained in the USA and had the privilege to attend MBI. As an MBI graduate, he had many opportunities open to him. This would not have occurred if Moody had chosen to ignore God's call.

Although, for many years communication was cut off by the political situation, David worked for CNEC [now Partners International] and managed their Shanghai office. In 1985, Partners found out that David was in Japan and they brought him and his wife back to the USA where he visited his friends.

One visit was to Chop Point Camp which was started by Peter Willard, who continued the legacy of his father, Rev. Wyeth Willard. During the Chens' visit, David's wife became ill and the Willards helped care for her. The Chens returned to Chicago where she died. Phone calls around the USA notified everyone and these earthly angels reached out to comfort him. After her funeral David returned to California and when Partners was notified that it was unsafe for him to return to China they helped him seek political asylum in the United States.

David learned at an early age that life can be unpredictable but you can always depend on Jesus. In the chaotic times in which we live, the world is governed by fear, greed, and man's inhumanity to man. However, the joy and peace of God's world is available to you by trusting Jesus to guide you through the trials of daily living. He is available every hour of every day. Jesus is not a particular church, religion or sect. Living for Him is a way of life.

Poor by the world's standards David believed in a God that always supplied his needs. During his life he continues to show us that simple deeds are all that are necessary. Through many trying times, David did not wait to be called to serve God but went out and served God in all circumstances. We encourage you to take this moment to accept Jesus and let him change your life forever.

David Chen and I challenge you to carefully read the lyrics of Phillip Telfer's song, "Pick You Up," "How can you say you don't believe in a life that you have never tried?"

"Pick You Up"

A question came from a friend of mine
"How can you say God doesn't let you down?"
"Where has God been all these days of my life?"
"All the pain, the hurt, the struggle all around"

Friend, there will be struggles all our days
God gives the strength to get through life and give us
     hope
And you might be tired of hearing His name
Jesus Christ the only key to enter through God's door

Chorus:

How can you say you don' t believe in a God that never
     let's you down

You've never run into His arms and let Him pick you up

How can you say you don't believe in a life that you have
     never tried

Won't you believe in Jesus Christ and let Him pick you up

I'm not saying life is full of roses
At least not life on earth as we see
But you don't have to be tangled in thorns
If you are then why not let God set you free

God wants to give us peace in this life
Peace of heart that nothing else can give
And when life on earth completes its time
Heaven bound with God is where true life begins

Repeat Chorus:

How can you say you don' t believe in a God that never let's you down

You've never run into His arms and let Him pick you up

How can you say you don't believe in a life that you have never tried

Won't you believe in Jesus Christ and let Him pick you up

Lyrics & Music By Phillip Telfer.

Become a BELIEVER

The decision to follow Jesus Christ is the most life changing decision you will ever make. For "What good will it be for a man if he gains the whole world, yet forfeits his soul? . . ." Matthew 16:26.

". . . I stand at the door and knock. If anyone hears my voice and opens the door, I will come in . . ." Revelation 3:20. Jesus Christ is knocking at the door of your heart waiting for you to let Him in. To receive Him:

1. **ACKNOWLEDGE** your spiritual need. "I am a sinner." ". . . for all have sinned and fall short of the glory of God, . . ." Romans 3:23.

2. **REPENT** and turn away from your sin.

3. **BELIEVE** "For God so loved the world that he gave his one and only Son, that whoever believes in him shall not perish but have eternal life. For God did not send his Son into the world to condemn the world, but to save the world through him." John 3:16-17.

4. Through prayer, **RECEIVE** Jesus Christ into your heart and life.

5. **AFFIRM** your commitment with your local church and seek guidance on how to grow in your faith. Now, "Do not be anxious about anything, but in everything, by prayer and petition, with thanksgiving, present your requests to God. And the peace of God, which transcends all understanding, will guard your hearts and your minds in Christ Jesus." Philippians 4:6-7.

Become an EARTHLY ANGEL

Many "Earthly Angels" started ministries before David Chen became involved with their organizations. He was one of the fortunate ones. "Earthly Angels" saved David from starving to death, allowed him to obtain an education, helped him to go to college, and taught him Christian values. We encourage you to become an "Earthly Angel" in any way that you can:

1. **PRAY** for the persecuted churches around the world.

2. **YOUR TIME**. Get involved with your local church.

3. **DONATIONS** are always needed to support the ministries in this book.
   Refer to the following pages.

Kids Alive International

Kids Alive is dedicated to fulfilling the spiritual, physical, educational, social and emotional needs of children and youth who have no other reasonable means of support. The long term goal is to win children to Christ and to prepare them to be Christian witnesses to their own people.

Children's Homes, schools, and care centers worldwide make it possible for Kids Alive to minister to children in Dominican Republic, Guatemala, Peru, Romania, Lebanon, Myanmar, Taiwan, and Papua New Guinea.

Kids Alive, formerly Home of Onesiphorus, began in China in 1916. The two Children's Homes in China were forced to close because of the difficult political situation. Later another Home in Hong Kong was closed. As times change Kids Alive plans to return to both Hong Kong and China.

Kids Alive welcomes people who love Christ and love children to serve as missionaries. Openings are available for career and short-term people in any line of interest (teaching, child care, vocational training, recreation, social work/counselor, and so on). Service teams are invited to spend time at Kids Alive ministry to do construction work, evangelism, and build relationships with the children.

Kids Alive cares for its children through the tax deductible donations of concerned people. In addition to missionary support and specific ministry contributions, Kids Alive relies on a Child Sponsorship program. The sponsor can choose a boy or girl in one of our countries and build a personal relationship with that child through correspondence. For $30 a month (just a dollar a day), the sponsor can make a significant difference in the life of a needy child.

Kids Alive International
2507 Cumberland Dr., Valparaiso, IN 46383
Phone: (219) 464-9035 or (800) KIDS-330
E-mail: kidsalive@juno.com
Web site: http://www.kidsalive.org

Moody Bible Institute

Moody Bible Institute (MBI) was founded in 1886, and is first and foremost a school. College and graduate-level work prepares pastors, missionaries and other church-related workers. Each of the schools' majors include intensive studies in the Bible and the application of classroom theory through practical ministry assignments in community organizations and churches. MBI also has a missionary aviation training school in Elizabethton, TN, evening schools in six states, a world-wide correspondence school, and a two-year undergraduate school in Spokane, WA.

In addition to its educational endeavors, MBI operates several other ministries. Moody Press publishes Bibles and Christian books, and *Moody Magazine* is published every other month as a Christian family magazine while *Today In The Word* is published monthly as a daily devotional guide. Moody Retail operates three bookstores and Moody Video produces videos for the Christian family. Through the Moody Broadcasting Network, MBI owns and operates 26 radio stations across the country, and provides network programming to more than 600 radio outlets across North America via satellite and to more than 400 additional stations worldwide via tape.

Moody Bible Institute continues to offer a tuition-free education to its students. Donations are tax deductible, and may be sent to the address below. Gifts may be designated to "tuition-free education", to "general ministries", or to any of the other ministries of MBI.

Moody Bible Institute
820 N LaSalle Blvd., Chicago, IL 60610
Phone: (312) 329-4000, (800) DLMOODY
E-mail: info@moody.edu
Web site: http://www.moody.edu

Partners International

Partners International, formerly CNEC, was founded in 1943. Partners is a recognized leader in partnering with indigenous Christian ministries in the non-Western world, linking resources from Christians in the West with Third-World agencies that minister to both physically and spiritually needy people.

The Partners team emphasizes local self-sufficiency and avoids creating unhealthy dependency. It works only with indigenous ministries that have proven track records. Its priorities are evangelism, church planting, grassroots leadership training and economic self-help.

Partners International currently provides financial support for 3,800 indigenous Christian workers in about 50 of the world's least evangelized countries, often in places where Western missionaries are not allowed. Every year these workers win about 50,000 new believers to Christ. They also provide many humanitarian services, train some 30,000 local Christian leaders each year and start an average of one new church–in an unchurched community–every eleven hours.

Gifts are tax deductible.

Partners International
2302 Zanker Rd., P.O. Box 15025
San Jose, CA 95115-0025
Phone: (408) 453-3800 or (800) 966-5515
Fax: (408) 437-9708
Web site: http://www.partnersintl.org

Chop Point, Inc.

Chop Point is a Christian nonsectarian organization founded by men and women who, through a well-balanced program of recreation, work and education, integrated with the spiritual dimension, encourage young people to choose worthy and unselfish goals.

In 1966, Chop Point became a reality when it established a summer camp for teenagers on fifty acres of beautiful land in North Woolwich, Maine. The camp is a teenager's dream vacation, where they can participate in such activities as biking, hiking, canoeing, swimming, sailing, kayaking, rafting, arts, & trips. There are two 3-week sessions each summer, which draw teens from all over the world.

In 1987, Chop Point started a private K-12 school, on the same property, that seeks to offer high-quality, nurturing, alternative education options to students who might not otherwise have access to such possibilities. The goal is to show young people that gaining knowledge is not drudgery but fun. A few of the current programs include: extensive horticulture courses taught in three fully-functioning and self-run greenhouses; an emphasis on teaching science and social studies by experience, from on-site archeological digs to local wildlife and nature studies; a cross-cultural program that teaches students Spanish (grades K-12) in preparation for a 3-week high school trip to Mexico or South America; and a boarding program for boys and girls ages 8-18. International students are accepted, enabling all students to receive an education rich in multi-cultural learning.

All charitable gifts are warmly welcomed, and are 100% tax deductible. Please mail to address below.

Chop Point, Inc.
420 Chop Point Rd., Woolwich, ME 04579
Camp Office: (207) 443-5860
School Office: (207) 443-3080
Fax: (207) 443-6760
Web site: http://www.choppoint.org

To obtain a list of available tapes or CDS:

Phillip Telfer
14826 Scenic Palisades Rd.
Mt. Carroll, IL 61053

(815) 244-4545

E-mail: **philliptelfer@internetni.com**

—

For information on the annual

"CONFERENCE
ON
THE PERSECUTED CHURCH"

in Columbia, South Carolina.

(803) 252-4146

AUTHOR

Phyllis A. Milkon

left the East Coast in 1988 and relocated to Oregon because it seemed like a wonderful place to write. Her first book, *Cooking Healthy* was published in 1991. *Earthly Angels* is the beginning of a series of Christian inspirational stories.

Writing projects and training materials have been a major focus of a business consulting practice that began in 1986. Her career also includes twelve years in banking as well as experience in other fields.

Phyllis attended the University of Pennsylvania's Wharton School of Finance and later graduated from Upsala College where she majored in English.